DANDELION CHILD

SANDI TARANTO

Sandi Taranto © 2018
All rights reserved.

CONTENTS

Dandelion Child	v
Caution & Important Author's Note	vii
1. Setting the Scene	1
2. A Promise (Sandi)	7
3. The Failed Houdini (James)	11
4. It Begins in Death (Sandi)	17
5. Darren Takes the Case (Darren)	25
6. Shocking Details (Sandi)	29
7. Of Predators and Prey (Darren)	35
8. Darren's First Visit With Sandi (Darren)	39
9. Bad Dog! (Sandi)	45
10. The Chase Begins (Darren)	53
11. Like Minds (Sandi)	59
12. Squalor (Darren)	63
13. A Bubble Bath- of Sorts (Sandi)	69
14. Sharing is Caring (Darren)	73
15. Pork 'N Beans! (Sandi)	79
16. Many Memories of Midnight (Sandi)	83
17. Missing and Ignored (Darren)	91
18. Keeping Her Place (Sandi)	97
19. Unexpected Ally (Darren)	105
20. The Boy (Sandi)	109
21. Burial Without Fanfare (Darren)	115
22. Into Darkness Again (Sandi)	119
23. Done Away With (Darren)	121
24. Afterparty (Sandi)	127
25. On the Dole (Darren)	131
26. We Meet Again... (Darren and Sandi)	135
27. Nobody Wants Them, Anyway (Darren)	141
28. Put Through The Wringer – Literally (Sandi)	145
29. Always a Local Matter (Darren)	149

30. Movie Magic (Sandi)	153
31. Darren Takes Score (Darren)	157
32. Rest and Reunion (Darren & Sandi)	161
33. The Calling (Darren & Sandi)	165
Q&A	169

CAUTION & IMPORTANT AUTHOR'S NOTE

In Sweden, there is a social tradition in which children who suffer horrible childhoods but thrive regardless are called "Maskrosbarn." Or in English, "Dandelion children."

Please don't read this book. I know, worst sales pitch ever; but that's because it's not one. This is a horrible, awful book. I get it, I wrote it, so I should be very proud of it, otherwise why write it? I'm not proud of this book, and I am, and have been since the beginning, deeply conflicted about even writing it. The writing is passable, but unedited. It was too hard for me to edit it, so I beg your indulgence on that front. It's not the writing that makes me conflicted, though.

I only wrote this book because I believe people should really internalize what it's like to be a tortured child. Too many of them are slipping through the cracks. We as a society are living our lives in complacent slumber, ignorant of or ignoring the children suffering around us. We must wake up, we must take the willful blinders off. We must do better. Children have feelings, too.

I was intentionally not graphic about the rapes I experienced. (I am purposefully not calling it 'sexual abuse'. I feel like that's softening language. If a man snuck into a child's room at night and had intercourse with them, it would be rape—unless it was a parent or caretaker. That should change, but I digress). Often I am asked what exactly was done to me. If you need to have it explained beyond "pretty much all of it", then you must find another source. I have chosen generally not to be explicit simply because I am not writing porn for sadistic pedophiles or opportunists here. I refuse to be explicit and knowingly titillate diseased minds. I know that the insinuations may be enough for some of them, but that will be all they get and even that for the sake of educating others, and for that alone.

Please understand that *only the part of the story that is about me or my mother* is "completely true and without dramatization" to the best of my memory. Other parts are dramatized as best I could manage from knowledge I gained, such as the part about James escaping and being brought back. I can't truly know what he went though that night, but I'm sure it was even worse than we can truly imagine. I have not knowingly included any falsehood in the story, I have been honest to the best of my ability in all of it.

The Detective's parts are a conglomeration of several people, most of whom wish to be anonymous. While the story doesn't follow his individual path with perfect historical accuracy, I have done my best to represent what I learned from the people who investigated or had knowledge of the case. I have not knowingly embellished beyond adding a few things that might make the reading more interesting but don't change the story's truth. I did initially try to make it considerably better from a 'story' standpoint, but realized I'd rather leave the unvarnished truth. The puppy story is the only part where I took liberty with "the Detective". Only for his part, not mine.

Those parts which specifically are about me (Sandi) or my mother should be considered as historically accurate as I can recall. Even then, some are repeat events told only once. There were many rapes, many episodes with the ipecac, etc. Most of these were not singular incidents even though you will read about them only a few times (with the exclusion of being forced to break the ice and bathe).

I did not go into the more common (but still sadistic and immoral) 'punishments' such as being locked in a closet or a small side table, whippings, being stripped and tied up outside to sunburn, the many beatings with boards, etc. I believe that the reader can only take so much, and this will already be an extremely savage ride, so I didn't go into every experience. I left so much out, but it's still grueling to read (and write).

One example that was left out and which is of interest is that every foster child's name was changed to whatever Doris wanted it to be, though she claimed it was to protect us from "stigma." That was a traumatic event for me, but I did not include it here. It should be noted this is a common element of the B.I.T.E. model of human trafficking. I have used my own real life name in this book in part as defiance of the name change forced upon me against my will as a child. I was at first given the option to have whatever name I wanted. I chose Elizabeth, so Doris forced me to accept Joanne, which I didn't like. This is just one example of many of the tortures listed in the B.I.T.E. model which were my everyday life (and for most if not all of the others, as well).

I beg you, if you read this despite my warning, please, please, please care for yourself lovingly. Do not feel obligated to finish it. Do take breaks. Do breathe. Do take warm epsom salt baths or even go to a spa. Have tissues nearby for the tears. And above all, if you can't continue, **_please stop reading_**!

CHAPTER 1
SETTING THE SCENE

NOVEMBER 1977 calls immediately to mind bell bottom pants, slug bug Volkswagens, tie-dye. These were the days of disco. It was a time when kids rode in the back of pickup trucks and smoked cigarettes and played outside. Gas had soared to a whopping sixty-five cents per gallon, and the average house was fourteen thousand dollars.

Some people had rotary phones still; while some reading this book won't even know what a rotary phone is. Cell phones and talking to someone on the other side of the world while at the beach was literally science fiction. It wasn't a thing of the future, it was a thing of whimsical imagination.

For the nerdy types, the Atari came out in September 1977. Advanced Dungeons & Dragons was all the rage. Dagorhir Battle Games was established to re-enact ancient battles, with all players required to be in character at all times. From Dagorhir would spawn countless role-playing battles and groups for decades still to come.

Music fans might remember that it was the year that Elvis died- or didn't, depending on whom you ask. If you were around back then, you probably heard Debby Boone's *You Light Up My Life* playing over and over through the day on the radio. It set a 10 week record at number one on the charts, remaining there all of that November.

Of course, let it not be forgotten that Star Wars came out that year. Forty years later, with new Star Wars movies coming out so frequently as of this writing in 2018, it would be remiss not to mention it. With a budget of eleven million dollars, it grossed seven hundred seventy-five thousand at the box office. It also launched a fandom that would resound through decades to come.

Mattel Electronic Football was more common than the much-desired Atari 2600. It was even portable! Ironically, you might have seen someone playing it while at a live football game. Hand held games were in their infancy, but they were immensely popular. It was the beginning of the transition into a digital world.

On the matter of sports, the Oakland Raiders put a beatdown on the Minnesota Vikings thirty-two to fourteen. In the last expansion of baseball until 1993, the Seattle Mariners and the Toronto Blue Jays made their debuts. The New York Yankees won over the Los Angeles Dodgers to take the World Series. Carlos Monzon retired undefeated as the World Middleweight boxing champion. Seattle Slew, out of My Charmer by Bold Reasoning became the tenth horse to take the Triple Crown. 'Slewmania' gripped the race-going populace.

Little of this, however, mattered to our little girl. She turned six in November of that year, and she had been in foster care with the Joneses for three years by that time. Her mother was in a heated custody battle with them by the time we reach the place where our story begins. In the end, beginning at age three, she would be with the Joneses a total of four years, being seven at time of rescue. But let's not get ahead of the story...

Like all stories, this one starts before our story here begins. Mitch and Doris were foster siblings of migrant farmers. The exact story of how Mitch came to live with Doris's family isn't known, but he was her foster brother. They married and moved to Emmett, Idaho.

They were considered to be devout Baptists, although Doris

ranted and raged that churches were wrong and evil. All anyone needed, she made it clear, was the Bible, which she alone truly understood. She was feared throughout the community for her flash rages, though she usually just threw things and screamed. Not dangerous, necessarily, people thought, just volatile.

Then she called the school and told a teacher's aid that she was going to "blow [her] away with a shotgun" for "putting the devil's mark" on one of her foster children. The teacher's aid had marked the girl's hand with "PTC", which was meant as a reminder of a Parent-Teacher Conference. The threat was followed up by a stream of enraged profanity.

Mitch, on the other hand, was feared as dangerous, there was no mistake about him. At the local mill where he worked, he was considered one of the hardest workers, and even if people feared him, they respected him. He had quite the work ethic. As such, people avoided him for his temper and lauded him for his exemplary efforts at his job. He was incredibly strong and sturdy, able to easily pick up large objects alone that other men struggled together to lift. He seemed to many to be larger than life, a thing of terrifying awe. It was "almost unnatural."

Their home outside of town was ramshackle and built by hand. Mitch had enough skill at hammering and sawing to make it get by, although not up to building codes, not even the lax ones of the time. By the time Sandi arrived, it had begun to show the ravages of time and of lack of care. The flooring inside the house was sparse. Where it was actually installed, it was so dirty that whatever had once been there—likely a wood floor—was now gray with the passage of time and with the presence of dirt.

A strange people, unused to a settled life, they kept habits which others considered strange, perhaps even bizarre. Inside the house, in the living room was where they butchered their animals. Hogs mainly, but also chickens. To those living there, this activity taking place within the house was of no moment, and few outside knew about it, though rumors abounded. Most people were not allowed inside.

The charnel pit where they butchered would be filled in and a new one dug on occasion. They used most of the bones, if they did not outright cook and eat them. What weren't used or eaten were thrown into the pit. A layer of dirt would be thrown on top of that. People found it most peculiar to see humans eating bones, similar to the way that a dog will chew up bones and eat them. Many didn't realize, until meeting the Joneses, that humans can chew up and eat small bones such as ribs. The Joneses disabused others of the notion that "It's impossible for humans to chew up bones" many a time.

The blood from butchering was a real problem, however. They didn't like to let the blood go into the charnel pit, so they would catch it in buckets. These buckets of blood often sat on the edge of the pit beside the hook used to pull the corpse to the side for gutting and slicing. One simply did not go into the pit whenever avoidable, but if anything dripped or fell, better into the pit than on the floor to require cleaning. In particular, people today would find this an offensive practice; this habit of having blood sitting around in buckets. It was considered creepy even at the time, though few would ever know of it because of the insular nature of the home.

Mitch got by with the house not being up to code by the simple expedient of running off any inspector who showed up to investigate it with a shotgun. Many of the electrical outlets were covered with duct tape, if they were covered at all. There were untreated beams in many areas, and if the house had any insulation whatsoever, it was unlikely anyone could have proven it. There were unfinished walls and unfinished floors; the only exception being Mitch's 'den'.

In the yard and inside the house in various places lay the detritus of forgotten dreams. They had been intending to run an electric fence for cows, and maybe even a horse. Year after year, the control box and the lines for the fence sat against the wall in the living room. It was duct taped to an outlet, since it came with raw wires rather than with a plug at the end. Their one attempt to install it had not gone well, so they had abandoned it for later, never bothering to disconnect it from the live wires of the exposed socket. "Someday," it seemed to say as it sat beside its outlet, staring out into the house in silent disinterest.

Rusty metal and other junk squatted in the corners and along the wall. An old hand plow rusted peacefully beneath the lucky horseshoe which hung crookedly above it. Eventually, the nail holding the horseshoe gave up and it fell, forgotten amidst the sea of unrealized hopes. A black wood-burning stove squatted balefully in the living room, watching the world with aloof cynicism. Not far from the stove sat a tiny black-and-white TV on a platform fashioned out of two-by-fours to be the right height for an adult to watch from the rusty metal folding chair in front of it.

Everything in the house seemed gray or brown, a bleak and uninteresting drab that dominated every single corner of the place as if a shroud covered it. What was clean, which wasn't much, was old and bleached by time until whatever color it might once have been could no longer be guessed.

From the outside, the house sat on a small plot of dry, dusty land. Mostly hard-packed dirt, it echoed the conditions of the interior. Large empty spaces were surrounded by piles of rotting wood, ancient farming tools, rusty metal, and broken-down equipment. A small, elderly tractor sat as a silent sentinel, peeping out from beneath a heavy sheet of aluminum roofing that had once graced some building or another. Nails poked through it still, threatening the unassuming old tractor should he stir from his reverie. Time and weather placidly gnawed at his bones, rust eating him in a slow, steady march that would continue for decades longer than the years when once he had proudly plowed land and hauled trailers.

Here and there, a forlorn tree attempted to rise from the hard dirt, reaching scrawny arms towards the sky in a mute appeal for water, or perhaps mercy. They rarely had leaves, even in the summer, and what few they did were small and hid little of the tree's twisted, desperate fingers.

It could have been almost anywhere in the USA, this two story home with its snuffling pigs, scratching chickens, and quiet, large-eyed children. Times were hard for many, and it was no different here. Great plans for the future were dying a slow but hard death in this place, as they often do for those trapped in poverty. More than plans were germinating here, though. Much, much more. The quiet exterior hid darkness and decay deeper than even the most aware of people could have imagined possible.

CHAPTER 2
A PROMISE (SANDI)

"Please, Momma, please. Take us and run away. Run away and we can live in the woods!" the words were slurred like those of a person with a significant mental impairment as the six year old girl pleaded with her mother, begging her to save her. She would later be diagnosed as low-functioning autistic. For now, she wore the simpler, crueler label of "retard".

The pair stood on the porch of the Joneses' rickety house. The red-haired woman squatted down, taking the peanut-sized blond's shoulders in her hands. "Be strong for Mamma. Can you do that? I'll be coming for you soon. So soon."

Threatening to buckle, the boards of the porch creaked under them as if protesting the possibility. Nearby, a piece of plywood once intended to block a hole in the wall clattered against the house, flapping as the wind tugged at it. The entire house groaned as the wind rocked it, oblivious to the tableau playing out on the porch. Above them, the brittle, overly bright sun watched indifferently from a sky touched by the cold of encroaching winter. The land held desperately to the dying embers of fall.

The only green remaining on the wind-swept property was the

dandelion plants. Their flowers gone two seasons ago, they none-the-less clung stubbornly to their chlorophyll, holding on to the bitter end. What little other vegetation remained on the property had given up weeks before, their brown corpses littering the ground in wretched abandonment of a life too fraught with hardship to continue on with.

The little girl shrieked and screamed, begging as her mother left. She sobbed uncontrollably, her fear and yearning bridled only by the hard arms of the woman she was forced to call "Mommy," who held her cruelly back from the leaving mother.

Yanked sideways by the hair, Sandi was forced to glance up into hate-filled blue eyes as Doris twisted her neck around. "You're mine. You'll always be mine. We'll kill anyone who tries to take you away from us. You understand? We'll kill them." She shook Sandi hard, her fingers digging in, leaving bruises in their wake... but they were lost amongst the multitude already there.

Beyond Doris, Mitch stared at Sandi with cold, unblinking eyes. Mitch's eyes were always cold, but sometimes, they expressed the hateful, virulent rage that typified his outbursts. This was one of those times. His full, bushy beard hid his full expression, but those eyes stole all need for guesswork. She barely glanced at him, for she had never done well with meeting anyone's eyes—and especially not Mitch or Doris's.

He nodded once and terror struck her silent. Tears rolled down her face as she was dragged inside the house. She could not look at him beyond that first glance which already told her too much, could not see those terrifying eyes. She stared anywhere else, wanting nothing more than for her mother to come back and take her away to...anywhere but here.

The door closed behind them, banging and creaking steadily in the same wind that toyed with the plywood over the hole in the thin wall. Mitch silenced it by lifting it and yanking it shut so that it finally latched, hinges protesting with high-pitched, desperate screams. He glared out over his domain before closing the interior door and turning silently into the dark, gloomy, filthy interior of the house.

Some time later, when Sandi finally could not control them any longer, her screams mingled with the howling wind, echoing late into the night. Doris's rages came in mighty, crashing waves, but Mitch's were long and his strength and endurance legendary in that tiny town.

CHAPTER 3
THE FAILED HOUDINI
(JAMES)

THE DARKNESS of night was deep, the moon hanging low in the sky as a mere sliver. A tiny figure crept slowly and carefully along the road, watching behind for expected pursuit. He resolutely turned back towards his goal. It was a far walk. It was late and he was deeply weary. He couldn't stop, he couldn't rest.

James's hip ached where he had been kicked. His stomach cramped from where savage fists had pounded it. His skin throbbed painfully from the weals left behind by the switch which had cut deeply into flesh. The night was too cool for sweat despite his exertions; the liquid running down his back was blood.

It was so cold, indeed, that his hands and feet felt like lumps of ice. His hands were curled as close to his body as they could get. He had tucked them into his armpits earlier, but that had simply sucked the warmth from his body faster and so now he held them against himself. His leaden feet had lost sensation a while back, but pins and needles had begun to stab relentlessly at them now.

His small legs wobbled. At 8 years old, it was hard going, the unpaved road uneven and visibility nearly nonexistent. There were no street lights here to light the way. Darkness pressed against him and he stumbled yet again. He still didn't stop. He couldn't.

He paused in his trek, shivering, arms wrapped around his chest tightly. There was nothing but pain and exhaustion. He moved forward, stumbling and tired. Sleepiness and pain warred with certainty that this was his only hope to escape. Desperation pounded at him, shoving him forward with such cruelty that he fell. He lay where he had sprawled for a moment, breathing raggedly. His hands were scraped from his fall. It would be so easy to just rest for a while. So easy. Desperation and hope together whipped him mercilessly and he climbed slowly to his feet.

He looked behind him, searching for pursuit. It always seemed as if Mitch and Doris, his foster parents, knew everything. If they didn't know he had escaped yet, they would know soon, he was sure of it. Panic welled despite the fact that there was no sign of the anticipated pursuers.

He had promised his mom that he would look out for his little sister. He would protect her, he would be the man of the family, no matter what the Joneses said.

The Joneses had told him that the pigs—the cops—would steal him if he ever spoke to them. He remembered otherwise from TV, though, and from school. They said the cops were your friends. You could trust them. They would help you, he'd been told. That was why he couldn't stop, why he couldn't rest. His and his sister's life depended upon him reaching the safety of the Sheriff's Office. The police served and protected people. There was safety there. He could not fail. All he had to do was reach them.

They would save him and Sandi. They would. He believed it with his whole heart.

It seemed hours later when he reached town and snuck behind houses and along walls and fences to reach the Sheriff's Office. There, he pounded on the door, looking around. Any moment, Mitch or Doris would show up and take him back. He had to get free. He had to. He had to get Sandi free. He had responsibilities. He couldn't stop pounding on the door, desperate need driving him to make them hurry, hurry, hurry.

The door opened. A sleepy woman looked down at him, her face going white as she took in his condition. "Come inside," she said, gently guiding him to a chair. She locked the door after looking around behind him much the way he had moments before, as if also worried about possible pursuit.

Her voice was muffled as she made a call from another room. She bustled back out to where he was, her manner excessively bright as she wrapped an overly large coat that smelled of perfume around his shoulders.

"You just sit tight, honey," she told him. "Everything is gonna be okay."

Across the room, she took out a can of condensed soup and poured it into a pot, which she placed on top of the old, black cast iron stove which burned cheerfully in the corner with its front end open. Wood popped and crackled as she chatted while she heated up the soup.

The scent of food made his stomach growl. He watched as she prepared it, babbling words he didn't listen to. She poured it into an ancient bowl as he watched. The faded blue paint was dotted with bright yellow flowers. Despite the age of the old clay bowl, and the crinkling of its paint, it was intact. It warmed his hands as she placed it on the table.

The dispatcher watched him as he fisted the spoon immediately, his frail, emaciated hand shaking violently. "Oh honey." She grabbed the crackers she'd placed on the TV tray she'd set up for him and broke them, putting them into the soup for him. "Stir those in. It's better this way. Give them a minute to soak up the soup. It's still too hot, anyway." She smiled, but choked on her words as she took his hand in hers to warm it for a moment so he could eat on his own.

She had raised sons and knew that his dignity would be shattered if she tried to feed him herself. He wouldn't be able to eat until the violent shivering had eased. When it had warmed between her palms, she released his fragile hand and made no further comment.

James tried to eat, but tears and sobs got in the way for several moments as he once more broke down from the combination of immense fear and intense hope. His hand continued to shake for long moments until he could get himself together. The dispatcher tried to hug him, but he couldn't bear to be touched any more than she already had. The soup was cool enough to eat by the time he was able to take a few shakey mouthfuls of it.

When the deputy whom the dispatcher had called came inside, James tried to tell him everything. Words tumbled out on top of more words. The soup grew cold as he talked, his ravening hunger taking a back seat to the need for rescue.

"I'll talk to the Sheriff. Wait here. Eat your soup. Everything's going to be okay. We'll make sure everything's okay, alright?" The deputy ruffled his hair and, reassured slightly by the gentle touch, James began to eat in earnest, gripping the antique bowl tightly against him with one hand while he used the spoon with his other, his face nearly inside the bowl.

When the deputy came back into the room, he was tight-lipped and his hands gripped his belt tightly. "Come on, son. Hop in the car."

"Why?" A terrible feeling rose inside James, and he dropped the soup as he jumped up from the chair. "Where are we going?" He already knew, though. How had he thought it would be this easy? How had he given in to hope? There was no escape, he knew that. Somehow, deep down, he had known that even before he'd begun this trek, hadn't he?

"Let him eat," the dispatcher begged, but the grim-faced deputy shook his head.

"Sheriff's worried. He told me to hurry and not to get myself shot taking him back there." He dragged James out the door and into the car.

James fought and struggled, trying to hold onto the table first, and then the door. As he was dragged out, draped over the deputy's shoulder, he saw the broken bowl lying in a puddle of bright tomato soup. The red of the soup stained the once cheery, if faded, yellow flowers. The lumps of cracker in the puddle of red looked like bits of brain to James, he having seen enough slaughtered animals to know the look of it. The soup spread across the floor as the door closed between James and the much longed-for safety of the Sheriff's Department.

In the end, James didn't have enough strength left to fight, so he gave up and was still. Minutes ticked by in the back of the police car as they drove. In the darkness, the house loomed over the car as they pulled into the drive. The headlights played on the porch, casting strange, terrifying shadows across the doorway.

The gnarled shadows of trees reached out from the darkness like crooked fingers, straining towards him in the light of the car's headlamps. The house groaned in a gust of breeze and the evil fingers seemed to wrap themselves around his very being and strangle the small spark of hope that had dared try to take root within him.

He was right back where he started. As he was ushered inside the house and the cruiser drove away, his screams and pleading took a long time to stop. The beating took much, much longer.

CHAPTER 4
IT BEGINS IN DEATH (SANDI)

THE TINY CREATURE hiding under the sideboard among the dust bunnies and assorted detritus stared out into the darkness in utter silence. She had learned the dangers of this world, and she knew that stillness was key, second only to quiet. She squeezed deeper into the shadows. The voices grew louder as the door creaked open, though she ignored what they said to focus on their location instead. Would they see her?

She wasn't to be up at night. She wasn't to get up even to use the toilet. She wasn't to soil herself or the bedding. She could not manage both this night, because her need was urgent. In her argument with herself, she had finally decided that risking the toilet was better than risking soiling the bedding.

Now, she stared into the weak, wavering pool of light created by the open door. From outside, she heard the sizzling crackle of the porch light fixture. Poorly wired as it was, the sizzle of electricity could be heard from her hiding place. The light in the hallway where the voices stood was clicked on, spilling into the room she hid in. She struggled to push herself further into the deep shadows under the piece of furniture she hid beneath, uncaring that against her back was an outlet with no cover, unaware of the danger the partially exposed wires presented her.

As she watched, Mitch came into the hallway to head up the stairs to the second floor, and in an instant, her world turned upside-down. For the bulk of those three and a half long years trapped with the Joneses, Sandi had prayed to Jesus to save her. She had begged, pleaded, bargained... and yet here she stayed, day after day, month after month, year after year. In time, she knew she wouldn't be saved. Jesus didn't care about people like her. She was bad, so very bad, and filthy, and worthless. No, Jesus didn't answer her prayers because she wasn't even a person. She was even more filthy and grotesque and worthless than real people. Mitch and Doris and everyone else told her so at every opportunity.

When her mother had come back, she'd had new hope. She'd hoped she'd be saved. Her mother would save her. Her mother, with the laughing eyes, the freckles on her arms, and the sun in her red hair... she would save her.

Earlier this night, Sandi had been awakened by a scream. She had tried to rush to the window of the second-story window she shared with her foster sisters to see what was going on outside. She knew even then that it was her mother. She was certain of it. Her heart had pounded with terror and a need to see... to know... a need that was not to be met.

Her foster sisters had kept her from the window, holding her bodily away even as they looked out the window from their height advantage; but Sandi had been convinced it was a human scream, despite their attempts to claim it was simply a mountain lion. Unable to return to sleep, she had snuck from the room at her first opportunity to go pee, and maybe to see her mother. Her aunt, she corrected herself. She must always call Marie her aunt.

Here, in the deep of the night hiding under a bench in the dirt, the remnants of old food, and bug carcasses, she saw her mother draped over Mitch's arms in what adults would have called the "bride-style," and she knew the truth instantly. They'll tell you that children don't understand death. Whoever 'they' are, they're wrong; at least in this case. She understood all too well. She did know that her mother was dead. She felt it to the depth of her soul. She knew that death was forever.

In that moment, seeing Mitch carrying her mother across the entryway and towards the stairs, she lost all hope. As an airlock venting to space, all hope was sucked from her, leaving barren cold in its wake. Her mother, in her teal green shirt with the creamy white wool-lined coat over it... dead. Her head hung backwards from Mitch's arm unnaturally, as did her arm, flopping carelessly, a forgotten and useless piece of string swinging grotesquely in a nonexistent breeze.

Sandi knew her mother was dead. It wasn't a doubt or a question, it was certainty. It was primal and deep and despair came in a cloud darker and deeper than the night around her. Her mother was dead, and with her, all hope of rescue.

The darkest part wasn't the death of hope, though. Oh no. No. The darkest part was that, in that moment, Sandi knew. She knew whose fault this all was. She knew who begged her mother to save her... she knew who got her mother killed.

"If anyone tries to take you away from us, we'll kill them." The words echoed in her head for the first time that night. Words that would haunt her in years to come. Words that would wake her the moment she drowsed. They would repeat decade upon decade, taunting her with the integrity of their promise. From that night, they were a litany, a mantra of self-blame. Even during the times later when she wanted to believe the whole thing never happened... still the broken record played in the vault of her mind; an endless echo through the years.

She had begged. She had pleaded. She had screamed. 'Take us away from here. Just run away.'

There would be no more freckles. No more sunlight. No more hugs or laughter.

No more hope. No more chances. Sandi had killed her mother.

She waited in silence until they left through the front door again and then crept out. Slowly, so slowly, listening with every ounce of her being. She started up the stairs... her mother was up there. Somewhere.

Dead.

oOoOo

Slowly, stopping to listen every few steps, Sandi crept into the room where the jars of food were kept on the second floor. She knew what she'd find here, but not where to find it. She searched, until finally her hands pushed against the bottom back of the pantry wall.

The board there at the back of the shelf fell forward, exposing the large cubbyhole beyond it. She stared, her hand getting smashed when the board fell on it but instantly forgotten in the shadow of the ache filling her.

Dead. Her mother really was dead. Eyes stared at her, eyes wrong somehow, strange and alien. Her mother's eyes were different now, staring without seeing. One cheek was bloody, a bone standing out in the midst of the open wound, but Sandi only saw that out of the corners of her eyes... What held her captive was her mother's eyes.

Dead, strange eyes that stared and stared and stared, not blinking, not aware, just there. They seemed gray, a bit wrinkly almost. Strange. For that moment of time, Sandi forgot to be careful. She forgot where she was and the constant danger. In that moment, the tremendous sense of loss and horror seeped into her deeper than the cold of the floor into her bare feet. In her mother's eyes, she knew death and she knew despair and she knew that no god and no mother would come for her.

Ever.

There would be no happiness for her or any kid that lived in this house.

Ever.

There would be no human food beyond the few tiny scraps of old stuff she was rarely given if the dogs wouldn't eat it. No nights away from here at her mother's house.

Ever.

Then the sounds at the front door came again, and with a patter of feet, she fled the room, followed by the cruel edge of reality. Death's visage would live with her for the rest of her days.

Sometimes, she would awaken in the deepest darkness of the night, too afraid to even scream. Decades later, her heart would still hammer, her breath come quickly, and her eyes rove the darkness in fear of what she might see. Not fear of her own death. No. Life was too cruel to grant her death.

And if there was a hypocrisy in her thinking that she would want to die, but did not want her mother to; she did not understand it.

OooOo

ONCE MORE, the tiny figure crept through the darkness. The cold November night fluttered the thin, dirty gray-white nightie she wore, so she gathered it close, afraid the slight motion would give her away. She tucked the torn white lace around the hem of it up against her belly and slunk forward. She took one creeping step at a time, not rising as one leg inched forward, followed by the next in a crabbing squat-walk that took her forward until she could see the source of the voices she could hear already. They were indistinct, muffled, too low for her to make out or identify.

At the edge of the house, she huddled against the corner, the forgotten cold seeping into her once again. The air was sharp with winter's warning bite as it nipped at exposed skin. She squatted further down to watch, wrapping her arms around her knees. An incandescent utility light lay on the ground, shedding a golden glow into the surrounding darkness. In that ring of warm gold there stood three people to the left whom at first she didn't identify to herself, while she recognized Mitch squatting beside Doris, who sat on the ground. Doris was sawing with an electric saw and she and Mitch were arguing in harsh whispers that were pitched loud to carry over the saw.

On the left, Sandi then recognized her foster brother Roy. The other two figures, she wasn't able to recognize immediately, as the light was not hitting them well and their shadows stretched long and thin into the darkness behind them to be swallowed swiftly back into the inky night.

She didn't know what she was doing there. She hadn't come here with a plan, she had been drawn here. Perhaps curiosity, perhaps some inherent knowledge of what she'd find; we may never know. She simply came and watched as they butchered in the deepest hours of the black night.

Methodically, they sawed and threw meat to the pigs, who squealed nearby, awaiting their treats as they always did when humans drew near. That alone was not particularly surprising; it was normal to feed parts to the pigs during butchering, though butchering outside was very unusual, as well as doing it at night. What happened next was not normal at all; not even for these people.

It was as she squatted there for what seemed forever, as the cold sank into her feet and the darkness drew around her that Sandi saw an arm fall into the pool of light. It flopped like a forgotten string... as a puppet tossed carelessly to the ground. It dropped from behind Doris's body, independent of her. Not her arm... Marie's arm.

Sandi huddled in horror, emotionally frozen and physically freezing. She knew. She always knew even as the years passed by into decades; that it was her mother's arm. Where that knowledge came from, she would not know later, but the certainty would never leave her. That moment was indelibly etched upon her in all its sheer horror. A deep wound was struck into her soul and a part of her was lost forever. Beyond the pain of lost hope, beyond the destruction of faith... what was lost in that moment, there are no words to express. Something undefinable and precious slipped away and would never return. A spark deeper than hope, deeper than love, beyond faith and reason and self-esteem. She no longer had any will to live.

She did not run away in that moment. How much longer passed by is not measured by the memory, but the next thing she saw was light coming from the distance. They saw it, as well, and began a frenzied rush to clean up what they were doing. For an instant, Sandi recognized the back figure on the left, but that was all she felt--a moment of recognition and she noticed that he had funny legs... She thought no more of it, self-preservation kicking in intensely to override the momentary sense of recognition.

She fled to the back door, watching her dirty, cold, bare feet as she held the dingy white lace with its embroidered yellow flowers above them so she wouldn't trip. The concrete steps and her bare feet and a dragging, torn bit of lace were the last memory she had of that moment and oddly took precedence over everything except the moment the arm fell into the light and realization took seed. The memory of her own feet fleeing her mother's dismemberment would haunt her absurdly as that moment fell away into history; never repeated... never ceasing.

CHAPTER 5
DARREN TAKES THE CASE (DARREN)

D ARREN LEANED back in his chair and stared at the man on the other side of the desk. Darren didn't know him personally, and the guy wasn't exactly the crème de le crème of society--even in Emmett; which was saying something. The problem was that the guy was making sense. The man had raised enough money to hire Darren- if barely. That alone was enough to make him feel compelled to take the case. If this loser had that much money and hadn't spent it on MJ or LSD yet, he was definitely serious.

"What makes you so sure she didn't beat feet?" The woman in question had a bit of a reputation around town for prostitution and heavy drug use. She was another person he didn't know personally, but small towns always talked. There was less privacy in Emmett than there was in an open field full of people.

Jimmy shook his head adamantly. "We just got married and we just bought a house, ya know. Ya think she bought a house so she kin run off? She wants them two little shits of hers back, man. Plus, the pigs found her car with her wallet and paycheck in it, ya know? Ya gonna tell me she left without them things?"

Darren sighed. Somehow, given the reputation of the pair, he had a sinking feeling that this was going to go to hell in a handbasket immediately. Cases like this always did. The Joneses, whom Watson was pointing to as the culprits in this situation were held in a strange light in their own right, too. They were considered by most to be upstanding Christians, yet at the same time, Mitch Jones instilled fear in otherwise seemingly sane people. The most common words used were "hyper fundamentalist".

He took the case, albeit reluctantly and with great discomfort. He decided he wasn't going to let this case consume his life. A hooker, a druggie, and a couple of kids who were likely better off... Only one way to find out, though.

As Jimmy left the room, Darren turned to pick up a softball he kept lying on his desk. He knew only a little of the Joneses. They had something of a reputation around town. He'd never spoken to Mitch, but then again, they also didn't run in the same circles. Mitch was a mill worker. Most mill workers, while decent men, were dirt poor. Every penny they made that didn't go into bills--late, at that--went to booze or drugs.

He decided that the next day, he'd go out to see them. If Jimmy was right, and Mitch had something to do with Marie's disappearance, well... he'd find out. Decision made, he tried to turn his mind back to writing up the briefing on the case he'd just finished.

Behind him, the radio, playing Hotel California by the Eagles reached the point in the song where the lead singer crooned, "You can check out... but you can never leave..." In that moment, a darkness came over him that he couldn't explain or understand. On some level, he felt like he was checking into madness by taking this case. Would he be able to leave?

On an uncontrollable impulse, he threw the softball at the radio. The radio squawked and fell, spinning on its cord an inch or so from the ground and screaming with static. Sighing, he reached for his cane and made his way over to it, the hip wound that would never heal reminding him once more that he was no longer the man he had once been. Still so young according to everyone else in the business and in his life, but already broken.

He stood for a long time after he set the radio back on the shelf. When the next song that came on irritated him also, he flicked it off with an angry twitch. The sound of breaks squealing, the sickening thud of the car hitting his motorcycle, the crunch of gravel, and the pain of the accident rocked through him again, scouring across his memory like a saw on a rough log over at the wood mill that was the town's financial mainstay. They called the grinder there The Hog and sometimes he felt like you could hear it for miles. Grinding and grinding and grinding.

Closing his mind to the remembered pain and misery of his accident, he hung his head. Every day, he dealt with the dregs of society. His father scoffed at him, reminding him that he was young, far too young to be so jaded. His profession had taught him that women weren't to be trusted and neither were men. People lied, and cheated, and stole. He knew that they murdered, too, but in Emmett? A town the very definition of small-town USA? He suddenly wanted to be back at the DEA, where trouble was normal but predictable, but that part of his life was over; his life's calling never to be answered now.

The hated cane that had reduced him to working for his dad instead of undercover for the DEA ignored him completely as he vengefully leaned on it with his full weight for a moment. He growled and decided it was time to take out some frustration. Leaving, he headed for home and his weights. Slamming a weight or two would release the tension if anything could.

Ignoring the twitch a slammed door down the road elicited involuntarily because every loud sound now seemed to remind him of that car hitting him, he got in his Mustang and headed out. The 'Stang's tires squealed satisfyingly as the relentless, strange energy pushing at him translated into a rapid takeoff.

CHAPTER 6
SHOCKING DETAILS (SANDI)

BRIGHT SPRING sunlight streamed down across the dusty yard as Sandi squatted in the dirt. She was aware of the others inside. Through the thin walls of the house, she could hear their voices in low conversation like a fly buzzing lazily against a window. The warmth of the day was pleasant, though her pale skin was beginning to grow pink from the sun's attention.

She crept a few steps closer to the back steps. Fear clenched her gut as she continued to watch the sun glitter off of the bright, swirled rock she held in her hands. It was so beautiful, this rock. Golds, oranges, yellows... they seemed to dance around each other in the pretty stone.

She stared at it ever more intensely. In the distance, a vehicle's engine droned. She cocked her head, listening to it. She was comforted by the sound because it was far away, and by the warmth of the sun. She was so very rarely warm. In winter, she was almost never warm. The tiny bit of warmth was soothing and gentle.

The pain in her bladder was growing too intense to ignore. She would have to brave the cold, smoky interior of the house soon. She rocked forward and backward, alternately putting pressure on the urgent bladder... a moment of discomfort, then relief. Relief, discomfort...

The need would not be denied, and at length, she crept slowly towards the back door. Inching forward, she listened as a lull came in the conversation inside. The tiny black and white TV in the living room clicked on. Despair burned at her. She was unlikely to make it to the bathroom without being seen.

She opened the door slowly, mindful of its squeak. She stilled, opened it further, looked at the precious rock. Rocks weren't allowed inside; not for her, anyway. Her fist unfurled, and she watched it tumble down her palm, along her fingers, and to the ground, where it lay in a graveyard of the old, dead brown bodies of dandelion plants.

She promised to come back and get it. After. If she lived. She probably would. It would be far too lucky to be able to die, and she never got good luck, or any good things. That was part of being worse than a dumb animal. Part of being a useless burden.

The door was open just far enough she could squeeze inside. She slid along the side of the door frame. If she got inside without it opening any further, the door wouldn't creak. She tried to make herself smaller, pulling the door against her such that it scraped roughly along her sunburnt skin.

Finagling herself almost inside, she stopped, trembling, when the door creaked. Her heart's thunder roared in her ears above the drone of daytime TV. Her breathing was harsh, ragged, and too loud. She sought to conquer it. They would hear. They would come and see her entering the house without permission.

Nothing happened. Long moments passed and she slowly pulled free of the door. She put all of her not remotely considerable power into not letting it bang closed, panting with exertion as she fought the rubber tie-down strap that they had hooked over the door and connected to the frame to pull it closed against the spring insects.

Creeping down the hallway, she saw that no one was currently at the TV. She slipped into the bathroom, rushing to the toilet. She had just let her bladder go when the door slammed against the wall.

"What are you doing in here?" Doris screamed. "I didn't give you permission to enter this house!"

Bladder still streaming, Sandi was yanked off of the toilet. She managed to get the stream of urine under control, but she was already damp from it. Doris hit her. She kicked her. She screamed.

Then the real nightmare started. Doris dragged Sandi by the hair into the forbidden area in the living room where the butchering happened. None of the kids were allowed there, so on an ordinary day, she wouldn't have gone. She had no interest in being there anyway. She had no way to know how strange this indoor butchering was, but she knew enough to dislike it.

In the corner of the room sat a box, plugged into an unusual wall outlet. This outlet was covered in tape. The box it was hooked to was, unbeknownst to Sandi at that time, the control box for an electric fence for cattle. It would be decades before she would be able to identify it, though she noted similarities in some movies many years later with torture scenes involving car batteries.

What she did understand in that moment though, in fact knew, was that this box was horrifyingly painful. Agony was on its way, and she was petrified. She fought, screaming, kicking, biting... anything and everything she could do.

To no avail, of course. No matter how terrified a child is, they are still just a child. In the end, Doris's rage won, as always it did. Her wrath and her strength compared to that of a starving, scrawny child prevailed as predictably as the seasons and the tides. Inexorable, inescapable.

Eventually, Sandi lay on the ground, wrapped in wires that held her arms against her body, one of them painfully up behind her back this time, the other with wire jammed cruelly between two fingers. It wrapped around her shoulders and all the way down to her feet.

Panting with exertion, Doris stood over her, laughing, exhilarated. She landed another kick on Sandi's ribs. "The more you fight, the worse it hurts, you little bitch!" she screamed.

Sandi began to pray. "Please, please, Jesus. Please save me. Please help me. Please, oh, please, God, don't let her do this." She would get in trouble if she prayed. She would get in far worse trouble if she dared not to. Doris liked the prayers, though they had never done Sandi any good, and never would.

Doris laughed derisively. "You really think Jesus is going to help you?" She sneered. "Jesus doesn't love you. Jesus isn't going to help you. He already gave you to me to save, because not even he can love you." She leaned down and grabbed Sandi's head by the hair, dragging her closer to the dreaded box. "Why doesn't Jesus love you?"

In spite of her terror, or perhaps because on some level she knew obedience was equally fruitless as resistance, Sandi still said, "Because I'm just a dirty animal."

"You're what, again?" Doris snapped, twisting Sandi's head. "What are you?"

Sullen, begrudging despite the impending punishment, "I'm just a stupid, dirty animal who's more trouble than I'm worth."

"That's right. Nobody but me can love you. I love you, but you can't pray to me. You can beg me, though. Go ahead, beg me not to give you your proper punishment."

Before Sandi could say a word, she hit the small metal switch that turned Sandi's world into a nightmarish horror of pain. Agony coursed through her. Doris had tricked her, evident as Sandi's body went rigid and her teeth came down on the edge of her tongue because she had been trying to answer. She had bitten it badly enough once that the doctor had stitched it, but this time, it was a small, yet very painful bite.

Sandi had no control over any part of her body. Forced rigid, the electricity coursed through her, setting her on fire wherever the lines touched and making her body tighten with both agony and the force of the electricity. Urine and feces were pushed out, tainting the death-scented air with a new stench.

Doris turned it on and off, taunting and mocking. When that became no longer fun, she let go of the switch to kick, punch, and scream. Finally exhausted physically, she went back to the switch. On, off... on... off...

They had once intended to turn part of the land into a pasture for a horse, maybe a couple of cows. They hadn't gotten around to it, so now the cattle fence control box lay usually ignored on the floor beyond the butcher pit. It was affixed to the wall, and nobody bothered to remove it since the outlet wasn't currently needed. The oversight made it easy for Doris to use it for her 'punishments'.

"Please, Jesus, I'll be good. Please, Jesus, just make it stop. I'll do anything you want, just please, please, make it stop." Jesus was silent as wave after wave of pain screamed through her.

Of course he was. Jesus loved people, and she wasn't a person. She was a worthless retarded dog that nobody wanted, not even Jesus. She would die, cold, alone, and miserable on this packed dirt floor... but only if she was really lucky.

She wasn't. Neither Jesus, nor death, came for her that day.

CHAPTER 7
OF PREDATORS AND PREY (DARREN)

"THEM'S BAD people," the farmer said, spitting his tobacco juice at a chicken nearby. The chicken protested and squawked away. Beyond the stray chicken, hogs snorted and grunted, packed into their small pen together and jostling for dominance. Their ripe odor hung in the air.

Questioning people was the part of the job Darren lived for. "Why's that?" He never needed to do much in these conversations because people wanted to be heard; all you had to do was really listen.

"My grandpappy beat my pappy. My pappy beat me. But you don't beat yer kids fer fun. You beat yer kids to teach them. Yer givin' guidance. Correction. You unnerstand?"

Darren nodded agreeably in order to encourage the man to keep speaking.

The hog farmer pointed his hoe in the direction of the 'people' in question, despite the many obstacles between his house and theirs. Broken down cars littered both yards, along with bits of ancient, rusted metal of unknown origin. A tree struggled to rise from the assorted 'treasures' of decades, if not centuries. "Them people beat them kids fer nothin'. It ain't right."

By the time the farmer had finished, Darren wasn't sure what to make of it all. He had listened to person after person talk about how 'great' Mitch Jones was. Then he had listened to every one of them describe how terrifying he was. Be on his good side, he'd give you the shirt off of his back. Get on the wrong side of him, and who knew what dreadful thing might happen?

Mitch had hurt people in fights, but very little else seemed to explain the abject fear that people had of him. Somehow, without doing much to earn it, the guy exuded menace and inspired terror. Men looked at each other furtively and spoke in low tones when Mitch's name came up.

One of the men at the mill had told him a tale of how Mitch warned people that he had killed before, and wasn't afraid to do it again. Apparently, when asked how he had done it and how he had hidden the bodies, Mitch had been quite forthcoming. Darren wondered if the man behind him knew that Mitch claimed to have fed people to the hogs squealing in the pen nearby. The mill foreman was positive about Mitch and praised his work ethic—and made no pretense about the fact that he was also afraid of him.

Some of the stories said that Mitch bragged about feeding the body of someone he had killed to "the hogs," and others said that maybe he had fed the body to 'The Hog,' the grinder at the mill. Had Mitch been talking about Marie? Frankly, Darren doubted it. He had a feeling that Mitch talked like that to people to scare them, to make himself seem somehow more intimidating. His few years on the D.E.A. had introduced him to many such toughs who lined their stories with kills that clearly had never happened. The Sheriff and his Deputies were adamant that Marie had run off, but Darren had a job to do here, so he was going to give Jimmy Watson and Marie's parents their money's worth.

Doris, on the other hand, was utterly crazy according to nearly everyone. She was sweet as pie one moment and ranting and raging the next. Some of her family even talked about her temper at previous family reunions. Others went so far as to say that they left if they saw her there. This, Darren thought, was the woman that the courts had given seventeen kids throughout the years—that they knew of, and if stories were right, that was only the recent house count leading up to the current crop of seven. Meaning a lot of people said seventeen was the last count, not the lifetime total. Only seven remained at the home at present. What had happened to the other ten, most of them physically handicapped, racial minorities, or with mental disabilities? He didn't know, and that wasn't his job; which was proving hard enough already.

From his research so far, "those people" were serial foster parents who took in 'unwanted' kids. On the surface, that seemed like a very caring thing to do, but coupled with the fear in which people held them, he wondered. In the stories he'd heard so far, the state was all too eager to hand off problem kids to anyone who would take them, without concern for the final outcome. Out of sight, out of mind, he supposed.

Darren turned the Mustang out of the farmer's drive and stopped in front of, but across the road from the house Jimmy believed his wife had disappeared into and never come out of again; not alive, anyway. He looked at it, parking blatantly on the side of the road and leaning against the Mustang, curious to see what would happen on this fine, chilly Saturday morning. A young boy came out and fed the two hogs in the pen near the road. Darren recognized him as the son of the woman he was searching for.

The boy, James, caught sight of him and bolted towards the back of the house. A few minutes later, Darren's prey exited the front of the house. Mitch walked out and leveled a sawed-off shotgun at Darren and his Mustang.

For just a moment, Darren almost wanted him to do it. For that instant, a fleeting thought passed that he might just be better off. Then he pushed the thought aside and stared the man down. Never lock eyes with a predator, he'd heard before. That was how most people saw Mitch, but Darren stared at him, not backing down... Let Mitch see what it meant to meet another predator. There was always a bigger fish, and even though Mitch intimidated people, Darren was taller and bigger physically. Mitch might scare people with made up stories, but Darren was the bigger fish this time.

Mitch preyed on children. Darren preyed on men like Mitch. Drug dealers, murderers... Men who destroyed the lives of other people needed to go down, and there were too few people ready to stand up to them.

Slowly, as seconds ticked by, Darren began to smile. It wasn't a nice smile. It was a 'satisfied cat who has his prey mesmerized' smile. It was a feline's sheer joy in preparing to leap in for the kill. Yes. Darren hunted men like Mitch. He was going to take this guy down.

They both knew it, too. Deep, distant instincts in their brains told each of them that they were predator and prey, and that size notwithstanding, Darren was going to hunt Mitch until it was all over. Now that their gazes had met, it was a matter of time and nothing more. It was something primal inside him that said he was going to win this.

The gun barrel quavered for a moment, then lowered. A vehicle droned as it turned and started up the road towards Darren. Darren stood there, smiling. He ignored the oncoming vehicle, unconcerned. The dirt road was small, but Darren didn't let that concern him. Mitch stepped back into the dark interior of the squalid house. The door closed.

Darren watched a moment longer and then got into the Mustang. He would be back the next day, and there would be no shotgun. The dynamic had shifted and nothing would be the same again for Mitch Jones. He had backed down. He was no longer at the apex in Gem County, Idaho.

Darren drove away for the moment. Let the man stew in his new status for a while.

CHAPTER 8
DARREN'S FIRST VISIT WITH SANDI (DARREN)

THE NEXT morning, Darren went back to the wretched, filthy house. He made his way up to the front door, with its crumbling porch that violated multiple safety standards before you even reached it, and slammed a fist heavily against the door. Each thud of his fist banged the ill-fitting door against the aged, rotting wood of the frame and a smell of rot and decay rose from it in small puffs.

The sun beat down on his back and a wood thrush sang nearby in the cool spring air. In the cocoon of the porch, dust and decay held sway, while the world beyond it was brightly lit and sharp.

Feet and shouting echoed from inside the house. A small, dirty child opened the door, staring up at him. He looked down into blue eyes surrounded by wispy blond ponytails and said hello. The urchin blinked. This was Marie's daughter, he remembered from the photo.

"Sandi?" he greeted her.

She shook her head. "You can't call me that," she whispered, the words slurred and difficult to understand, as if she were talking slowly past food in her mouth. "You have to call me Joanne." Voices and steps came from beyond her, and she bolted away, scurrying and dodging around the few bits of furniture that got in her way, and other obstacles that lay strewn on the floor. Tiny ribs showed under the over-sized shirt she wore and her hip bones protruded visibly. Rage boiled inside him, but he suppressed it to turn to the woman who stomped angrily toward the door. The stench that had come from the door was magnified many times in here, the scents of death, rot, decay, and cooking food mingling in a fashion that made his stomach protest.

Her eyes narrowed on him. "Whut do ya want?" Her voice cracked like a whip, snapping out into the room and making the two children clinging to her hide behind her.

He walked into the house, knowing that she would do her best to keep him out, and she would feel vulnerable once he was in 'her' domain. "I'm investigating Marie Watson's disappearance. I'm going to need to talk to her children." He said 'her children' on purpose to antagonize the woman. It worked.

"Well, you can't. They's mine now, and I says no!" That voice snapped again, waspish and demanding. She expected her way.

Darren intentionally crowded her, using his bulky, muscular body to make her feel cornered. Despite her bluster, she was a woman used to being controlled, likely even terrorized. While he didn't think well of himself for doing it, he wasn't above using that to his advantage, particularly after seeing the state the children were in.

He gave her a cold, hard smile. "I'll just get a court order then. I'm sure Mitch will be happy when I come back with the Sheriff and a couple of deputies to help serve the papers. We could bring the custody filing at the same time. The one that gave Marie custody of her children." It was an empty bluff. The custody award no longer mattered since Marie had taken off, or gotten herself killed.

Doris's eyes darted around as her hands wrung in the kitchen towel she had shoved through the elastic of her pants as a sort of apron. The grungy towel might have been pink once, he thought idly.

"Fine," she snapped at last. He felt no relief, he had never questioned that she would give in.

"Alone."

She huffed and puffed and argued. Then she screamed. He let her carry on, waiting impassively, his arms crossed over his chest and his eyes boring into her. Nothing he said would convince her, she would have to vent her spleen and come to the conclusion herself.

Finally, the wind falling from her sails, she stood staring at him. He took one step closer with his good leg, the cane dangling from his hand.

Chest heaving, she trembled in rage. Insight rolled over him and he realized she wanted to hit him. She was abused, as well, he recognized, but he could feel no pity for her. She took her own anger and trapped feelings out on these children, he'd bet his life on it.

Once more, she spat, "Fine." She turned her head, her eyes on him, and screamed for the two kids. The girl came in behind the boy some minutes later.

"That girl ain't right in the head, ya know. Nobody wanted her, only me." At his cold look, she repeated, shrilly, "She ain't right in the head! She's a retard. You'll see!"

He walked into the other room with the two children. The boy chattered at him happily, as kids were wont to do. He didn't much care for kids, really. Loud, annoying, needy... but at times his work required him to find the patience and so he did.

He tried to warm the boy up, but the kid artfully dodged every question Darren asked. Frustration grew until at last he sent the 8 year old off to play. Turning, he saw the little girl tucked into a corner of the room wedged between an armoire and the wall. She was rocking back and forth, her head thumping against the wall behind her in rhythm to soft, nearly imperceptible humming.

This one, he realized, would be even harder. He had heard Doris say the girl was retarded, but somehow, he didn't think so. There was something in her eyes as she looked at him, something ageless and wise that didn't fit with a child; and certainly not with a child of limited faculties.

He dug out a notepad and a pencil. He liked to sketch, he always had. Kids liked Disney characters, so he had made himself reasonable with their sketches. He started with Mickey. Finishing the figure, he held it up towards her. "Do you like Mickey Mouse?"

She stopped banging her head and looked up at him. She shook her head 'no' slowly, saying nothing. He placed the pad down on the desk again and continued drawing other figures. After a few minutes passed, he saw her sneaking along the wall, and soon her presence was at his elbow.

She pointed timidly at the paper. "Who's that?" Her voice was heavy, slow, and slurred. She certainly sounded retarded, but he still wondered. Even if she were retarded, she deserved better than how she was being treated.

"That's Goofy."

She pointed again.

"That's Donald Duck," he said, using Donald's quacking voice. Her giggles warmed him.

At the same time, his heart was sad that she had no idea who Mickey, Minney, Donald, and Goofy even were.

At last, he asked her a few questions about her mother. Her eyes grew huge and she stared at him. "I can't answer that," she finally whispered in her slurred voice. "I can't tell you nothing."

He knew he would get exactly that from her; nothing. He sighed and tore the page off. "Do you want to keep this?"

Tears welled in large blue eyes. She gazed longingly at the paper before shaking her head. "I ain't allowed to have stuff and things. People keep things. I ain't a person." She scurried into the corner, her head dropping against the wall with a hollow-sounding 'thud' that repeated over and over again in a rhythm similar to a heartbeat.

He couldn't stand to be there a moment longer. He couldn't stand for her to be there a moment longer. He fought the rising need to grab her and run out of the door and hide her somewhere. He couldn't, he knew that rationally. It would only be worse for everyone; and especially for her.

"Hold on, darlin'," he whispered to her. "Help is coming. I promise I won't leave you in this hellhole."

Her head thudded against the wall again. He left, pain and heartache dragging at him with invisible chains. Every step felt like lead was dumped in his feet, and for once, he was grateful to have the cane.

Without realizing, it was in that moment that he truly accepted the case. It wasn't when he agreed to it, or even when he accepted the money. It was now. Here. It was with the realization that this tiny girl didn't even think she was human. It was beyond bearing.

The Mustang's engine rumbled to him of the future. He knew where he had to go, and what he had to do. He would make these people prove they had the right to even have those kids. He'd force a legal claim out of them, if--and he doubted sincerely--they had any. He was no rookie like Marie's lawyer. He was experienced. He'd been working with his father before the Academy, and he'd listened long before that.

A writ of Habeus Corpus would be on its way as fast as he could get it. He would give them a legal demand to prove they had a right to those kids. Even they wouldn't be able to ignore a court order.

CHAPTER 9
BAD DOG! (SANDI)

IT WAS CHRISTMAS, and the people were opening their presents in the living room. Sandi, of course, wasn't a person, so she had nothing to do. The good part of a major holiday was that she was typically free of the standard abuses for at least part of a day. No being locked in the closet. No cigarettes or cigars put out on her arms. No being chained outside overnight like the other worthless animals. On holidays, they didn't even lock her in the end table.

Not that their Christmases were what most people had, anyway. Even if she hadn't been 'less than human,' her holidays still would have been cold and barren. The family didn't "do" mainstream Christmas, so there were presents of needed items and there was a big meal. No Christmas trees or Santa or any other such 'secular nonsense'. Still, she was aware that she got nothing. Not a present, not a morsel of the fun foods.

Once in a while, some defiance would arise in her, an irresistible urge to have something she wanted. Holidays seemed an especially difficult time for her to get through.

She tiptoed her way into the kitchen where the remains of dinner lay cold and forgotten on the table. The other dogs were in the living room; they at least could be still and quiet. Although she knew intellectually that she wasn't a dog, she had become so used to being called one that she simply accepted it. After all, she was told, at least the real dogs were useful, unlike her.

She'd seen the dogs get away with stealing food sometimes, and this was her own chance, she hoped. She slunk under the table, feeling along the edge from underneath to find where the specific plate she wanted was.

Cookies. There wasn't much left, all of them broken, but Sandi wanted at least a small taste of a cookie beyond a crumb. Her hand grasped the plate, inched onto it... found gold. Bringing the precious piece down, she shoved it into her mouth and ran for the hallway.

Too late. Far too late. Her eyes met Doris's as the woman stared in hatred, eyes blazing with fury. Doris rushed forward, and Sandi desperately tried to swallow. The huge lump of cookie, still dry and not fully chewed, stuck in her throat and she gagged.

Doris's hand came down with brutal force, and Sandi rolled across the room, her small body slamming hard against the leg of the table and a chair. Abruptly halted by the furniture, she coughed spasmodically.

A foot hit the side of her head and she gagged again.

"Spit it out, you fucking little bitch. Spit it out or I'll kill you." Doris shook her hard. "Do you know what today is? It's Jesus' birthday, and you're ruining it by stealing. 'Thou shalt not steal,' that's a commandment. You're a filthy, worthless, stupid sinner. Nobody loves you, nobody wants you. I'm going to kill you for stealing that, you fucking little bitch."

Terror boiled and Sandi rolled over, trying to spit out the offending cookie matter. It stuck to her mouth, trapped by spittle, finally moist enough to cling stubbornly. Doris grabbed her face, forcing her jaw open by clamping her fingers on each side, and stuck the fingers of her other hand into her mouth. Cookie was scraped out.

Letting go of her face, Doris grabbed Sandi's hair in her fist, uncaring that it felt as if it were being torn out. She dragged Sandi down the hall to the bathroom, where abject horror took hold.

Sandi squirmed and started fighting, knowing exactly what was coming. It was always the same when it came to food. Doris yanked a cabinet open and pulled out the ipecac. Immediately, fighting became desperation, and Sandi clawed, kicked, bit, and fought with every tiny ounce of her pitiable 'strength'. Ipecac was a thing of nightmares. That bottle alone was enough to turn Sandi into a spitting, hissing ball of abject, unthinking terror.

Doris's hand came around her throat, and Sandi tried to scream as her air was cut off. She kept fighting, clawing and writhing with everything she had in her. Life narrowed to the need for air. Fear and pain and horror bloomed together into a dark cloud that closed around her. Together in her mind was the need for freedom and the desperate need to breathe. If she opened her mouth Doris would pour in the ipecac. She couldn't stop the need to fight.

Somewhere, dimly, she knew it would all be better if she died. Yet she couldn't prevent herself from struggling. She couldn't stop the darkness, she couldn't breathe--she couldn't breathe! Bone-deep weariness pervaded her and she could no longer struggle. Doris's face faded away into the distance until it became a mere pinprick of light at the end of a dark, dismal tunnel. Never would she hear "There's light at the end of the tunnel," in a positive way.

Then light and sound roared back as she convulsed and her mouth opened to take a breath, swallowing the ipecac instead. Pain wracked her lungs and burned in her body, her neck screaming its protest from the rough treatment silently as she coughed, shuddering again and again, searching in vain for great breaths of air that only brought agony and more coughing.

Then, just as her lungs began to work, the horrible wretched taste of ipecac made itself known. Burning through her mouth, it tore into her and stacked on the sensations of choking on liquid. The burning pain was so great that she tore at herself, trying to be free of the pain and the taste.

Doris laughed. "Thieving little bitch. What do you think happens to thieving little bitches in this house?" She dragged Sandi's head up, forcing her to look at her. "You're the most useless thing I've ever seen. You think you deserve cookies like real people? You'll pay for what you did, thieving bitch. Today is Jesus' birthday. You've ruined it for everyone. You're going to hell, with the rest of the sinners. You'll pay for this." Doris picked her up and threw her forcefully into the ancient, claw-footed bathtub and slammed the door as she left.

And pay Sandi did. The ipecac syrup did its work, and she soon began to vomit violently. The horrible taste was that much worse as it worked its way back out. Her chest heaved and her stomach heaved and pain burst through her in waves. She couldn't stop vomiting as her muscles protested painfully, her stomach and chest becoming sore from the force of it.

It didn't stop. It went on and on. Fatigue and strain dragged at her, as her body attempted to expel something but had nothing. Retching and retching, she lay in her own vomit, spittle and bile running down the side of her face as she convulsed again and again. Ipecac doesn't stop when the stomach is empty; it carries on until the dose runs out in the body, not the stomach. Thus the violent, convulsive retching went on and on.

She heaved so violently that she lost control over her bowels and bladder. The stench of vomit combined with the raw sewage of her own misery. The pain and exhaustion ripped at her, but it was only the beginning.

She wanted to die. She wanted the pain to end. It marched on, and she felt her heart hammering in her chest. Weakness and pain came together and she retched so hard that her head slammed against the tub, resounding like a gong. Stars exploded in her vision, but they didn't matter as she retched again, and again, long past the point where pain had become her entire existence. Like Prometheus chained to the rock, the eagles came and tore and clawed and devoured her entrails over and over again without pity or remorse.

In between bouts of vomiting, she stared at the strange patterns woven in dirt on the ring around the tub. Sunlight filtered in through the high window, and she stared for a moment at the motes of dust spinning around in it, the strange weaving of dirt their distant background as her eyes refocused. Then the pain came again, and soon the light, with its dancing motes, had crawled away across the room.

Was it hours or minutes later? She didn't know. Doris came in, forced her out of her clothes and forced her to clean the tub and her filthy clothes. As Doris hit her and kicked her again and again, Sandi barely noticed anymore. She lacked the ability to cry. She lacked the ability to respond.

She was humiliated. She was ashamed. She cared nothing for the cold water she was doused in to clean the urine, feces, and vomit from her and the tub at the same time. Her body was miserable. Her heart was hammering. She was exhausted. She hurt, both in her body and in her heart. Shame, fear, pain, hopeless, helpless, and impotent rage each took a moment to visit her, but in the end, apathy and hopelessness stayed while the others took their rest.

Eventually, she found herself lying at the foot of the bed in her designated spot on the hard lump of rags on the floor. As ever, despite the horrific exhaustion pulling at her, she slept lightly, awakening often. The night was no safer than the day.

oOoOo

"Please," Sandi pleaded, "I need to pee." Her hands were between her legs, trying to hold back the flood as she danced back and forth, facing the wall.

She was in 'time out' again. She had been there for hours. Breakfast had been eaten, lunch had been eaten, and still she stood. She hadn't even had her dog food yet today.

Doris once more screamed at her for trying to get out of her punishment. Mitch walked by and punched her in the head, telling her to shut up. As she flew into the wall, she could no longer hold back the urine. The floor flooded with yellow liquid and she shrank away in terror. She tried to run, a rare occurrence since that typically made everything worse.

"Stupid little bitch pissed herself," Mitch snapped.

Doris ran into the hallway. "I'll deal with it."

"You'd fucking better. I'll send the little bitch to the fucking pound if you don't." He kicked Sandi for good measure, where she lay sprawled from him catching her and throwing her to the ground.

As he walked away, Doris yanked Sandi by the ever handy hair, first mashing her face into her pee while screaming at her, then dragging her to get the mop and its bucket. Swearing viciously, she filled it with water and made Sandi clean up her mess. Of course, her work was inadequate as always, and Doris lost her mind when she saw that the mop water was now more on the floor than in the bucket. Sandi had tried to wring the mop, but the mop was large and her hands were tiny.

Dragging her yet again by the hair--a favored pastime--Doris took Sandi to the water behind the house. Frozen over, it was thick enough to walk on easily. Thrusting a heavy sledgehammer into Sandi's hand, Doris demanded she break the ice.

20 pounds was far more than Sandi could lift. It just as well have been a thousand, and of course Doris knew it. What followed was a tirade about weakness, worthlessness, and the inevitable reminder that retards aren't even people. Jesus rewards hard work—The Lord helps those who help themselves, and that's why Sandi would be nobody forever. A worthless burden upon the world. A burden upon poor Doris herself.

Doris, in her heavy winter coat, broke the ice and shoved Sandi in, clothes and all. "You wash the piss out of those clothes or I'll kill you." Sandi tried, but the freezing water made her numb and clumsy immediately.

Then, she slipped and fell under the water. Her head hit the ice above her as she tried to regain her footing, sliding on the bottom where mud slept over the icy ground beneath it. Doris's hand reached in and caught her by the hair, dragging her out.

She lay on the ice, coughing so hard water flew out of her nose and mouth both. Shivers slammed through her body, but she still wasn't clean enough. Held by the hair, she was dropped back in and dunked repeatedly under the water. Her lungs and body burned from cold and pain and the need for oxygen. Needles of cold stabbed her everywhere. She once more fought for a life she didn't really want at all, with the last of her waning strength.

When at last she was brought out, she couldn't walk, even to avoid the kicks, punches, slaps, and even bites Doris wasted trying to force her to. At last, still dirty with mud and shaking violently, she was dropped inside the back door, warned to clean up or face the consequences. She crawled until she could walk, teeth banging together in an unstoppable chatter that grated on her in the midst of her misery. She did her best to clean up in the bathtub, shivering in the cold water that was all she was ever allowed to use.

CHAPTER 10
THE CHASE BEGINS (DARREN)

DARREN SAT IN the Sheriff's Department, waiting for the big man, himself. William McConnel had been Sheriff since September. Darren had papers for him to serve. The writ of Habeus Corpus meant that Mitch and Doris had to prove they had legal rights to have James and Sandi in their custody. He was absolutely certain they wouldn't have any. Additionally, the Sheriff had a warrant to serve on Mitch for raping one of the other foster girls in the home. Putting Mitch away would be a happy addition to today's work.

The best part was that the grandparents--Marie's parents--had added to the payment for finding Marie and getting the kids out of the home. They had family to go to when he rescued them today. He could keep his promise and be home by dinner, if they could get going already.

He sat waiting for the Sheriff to return, but the radio burst with static, instead. He was asked to go with a Deputy, and they headed for the house in a squad car. The news wasn't good, but the Deputy said nothing further.

When they arrived, Darren's stomach immediately felt queasy.

Something was wrong. The neighbor from the hog farm across the way was shoving the two hogs into a pickup truck with the help of several young guys.

Ignoring them, Darren headed straight to the door of the house. As he lifted his fist to knock, the neighbor yelled at him, "Don't bother. They ain't there, ya know. They beat feet sometime last night. Called me and tol' me to come get them pigs this mornin'."

Darren pushed on the door at the Sheriff's call from within and it creaked open like something from a crappy old black and white movie about werewolves or vampires. The dark interior clashed with the sunlight of the chilly spring day, leaving him blinking and uncomfortable. The smell that rose from inside was offensive. The air was cold, no rush of warmth from a lived-in home slipping out.

He exchanged looks with the Sheriff. His prey was gone. He clutched the papers in his hand tighter. He wouldn't be rescuing that tiny, frail, starving little girl who could barely speak. Not today, anyway.

"I'm not a person," the words echoed through the cold that beat through the house like a distant drum. Piles of filth and residue of old meals sat in the kitchen. The charnal pit hadn't been covered and bones and piles of entrails lay in it, grotesquely still and silent. Buckets of drying blood sat beside it. They had butchered something before they left, an activity they performed inside their house. Even by Emmett standards, that was weird and creepy.

Bile rose and he stepped out of the door before it could be set free. The rank smell of fresh butchering lingered in the house, despite the cool temperatures. The stench of old death and rotting things set the backdrop--it was a smell he remembered well from his last visit. He supposed that if you lived in it, you got used to it, though he didn't know how you possibly could.

The young deputy, his stomach weaker than Darren's, lost his breakfast, heaving repeatedly and convulsively. Even after he was finished, his face was contorted and his hand shook.

There could be clues inside that house of horrors. He turned to look at it. It was open, unoccupied. It wasn't really legal for him to go inside; the writ was to be served for Mitch and Doris to hand over proof to be presented in court. Looking through the house wasn't exactly in its purview.

But the door was open. He went inside again to search, and to his dismay, found nothing that gave him any clue at all where they could have gone. Everything had just taken a horrible turn for the worse. His prey was in the wind, the kids he was to save were with him, and Darren could do nothing.

"Shit." He blew out a huge breath. He would have to ask his dad for advice. He loved his dad, and the man was savvy... but he didn't take kindly to dependence. Darren would get a lecture before he got help.

Groaning with frustration, he made his way carefully to the cruiser and rode back to town. Hell had just reached out her hands and taken him by the balls. Fury burned in him. Mitch was going to go down. He had looked into the eyes of several desperate children, and those eyes followed him into the darkness of the night. They cried out to him in the light of day.

He didn't realize he had forgotten the sound of crunching gravel, screaming brakes, and sirens. Now he remembered only the sad sound of a barely comprehensible voice asking him who Donald Duck is. Donald Fucking Duck... what kid didn't know who Donald Duck was?

It was almost as if that single, corny injustice became the mantra of his need to save those kids. It pushed his will, drove his mind, and gave him the courage to beard his old man and ask for answers.

oOoOo

Summer was already in the air when he finally found his first lead. He'd been trying to find out which way they had gone. Widening his search, he had crossed the Idaho border into Oregon and stopped for gas. As he always did, he pulled the photo out of his pocket. Dog-eared and tired, it showed Jimmy, Marie--the top of her head cut off by the camera--and the two kids. He showed the attendant on duty the photo. "Have you seen these two kids?"

He scowled. "Yeah, that one knocked over a display case," he said, pointing at Sandi in the photo. "Stupid kid. Just because you're a retard don't mean you can destroy whatever you want."

Darren stood staring at the man for a long moment. Did he really not understand what he had just said? Not that he was convinced she was retarded anyway, but he seriously thought the guy didn't understand the concept.

"Are you absolutely certain?" He didn't really need to ask; after all, it was clear the man had seen her and been told she was 'retarded'. That was far too specific to be coincidental.

"Yeah, man. She's trouble, you know?" The attendant went back to reading his magazine, ignoring Darren once more.

Darren didn't care. He had a direction. No one else cared at all. There were no leads coming from the Sheriff. He had shrugged, simply saying, "good riddance to bad baggage" when informed they were gone.

But what baggage? All of them, of course. Every last one of them were just trash to most people. From listening to people around the town, to everyone else, too. More people were glad the whole lot of them were gone than cared why they'd left, by a significant measure. The only exception was Mitch's boss, apparently the guy was a good worker.

He sat in the Mustang, breathing deeply for a moment. He was going on a road trip into Oregon. He was weeks behind already, and a sense of pressure had settled over him. He had no idea how he'd find them, but he looked at the photo of the two kids, and thought of the other two they'd taken with them, as well. To each and every one of the four, he vowed, "I will find you. I won't give up."

In that moment, the promise was made with certainty, but in months to come, the gravity of the promise would settle upon him like the wings of a demon shrouding all hope from his view. The vow took root in his heart and he turned the key in the ignition, pulling smoothly back onto the road towards home.

It was a long drive, with a lot of time to think. He had to get into the man's head. If he were Mitch Jones, where would he go? What would he do? How would he survive? Mitch had worked at the mill; he would take on manual labor wherever he went. Finding jobs that paid cash would be the first place he'd look.

His mind full of the chase, Darren settled in and pushed the Mustang faster.

CHAPTER II
LIKE MINDS (SANDI)

SANDI SQUATTED under the huge truck the workers were using to move logs. It was cool there, while the day was hot in the sun. There was so much room under the truck that she could squat there without even ducking her head, though the steps on the side of the truck were low enough that she couldn't see anything past them except feet and the bottom of trousers.

Beyond the truck, Mitch and two other loggers were taking their break, relaxing against several stumps their own work had conveniently provided for them.

"She's a purty little thing," one of the men said to Mitch.

"Yeah, dumber than a double-assed dog, though," Mitch laughed in response. "Don't need to be smart to suck a dick, though, if you know what I mean."

The man who had spoken, and the second one grumbled 'sick fucks' and walked away, leaning on a tree away from the others. Sandi watched him go, her eyes tracking him; a mouse watching a cat from the safety of her mousehole.

Mitch's voice called after him, "Don't come knockin' if the van's a'rockin'!" Sandi didn't know it meant that the pair remaining behind had just announced their intention to rape her, but she didn't need to understand the phrase to understand her fate. It was common enough in her life.

Mitch and One continued talking, their tone and their words coarse and mocking. Familiar with the tone, though not truly understanding on any conscious level, Sandi eased back deeper into the truck's shadow.

She picked up a yellow flower from beside the gravel road, turning it over in her hands. Moving over to the far side of the truck from Mitch and One, she found a patch of sunlight that filtered past the truck to land beneath it. Holding the flower up, she studied its cheery yellow face.

It was beautiful, that flower. She touched it, feeling the texture of its petals. Beyond the truck, Mitch and the other man's voices continued, causing a coil of fear to wrap around her stomach. She pulled tighter into herself, focusing on the flower, trying to make the whole world disappear until there was only the bright yellow of the flower. So pretty...

"Why ain't she in school?" Two asked, his voice coming closer.

Sandi curled up on the ground, face out of the light, rock still clutched in her hand and held in the pool of light. Focus, focus... close everything out but the pretty rock... Hide, disappear. She tucked further into the truck, hoping they wouldn't see her or realize she was there.

"She ain't old enough for school yet, besides, it's summer, ain't it," Mitch's voice was also coming closer.

They began circling the truck, taunting her, telling her in coarse terms what they were going to do to her and what they were going to force her to do. Sandi wasn't innocent. She knew exactly what they were saying. This wasn't the first time she would be savagely raped. At the age of 6, she'd been a sex slave for years already. Rape was no new thing to her.

What they were saying did its job; it struck fear inside her. They were laughing, taunting, mocking. Next, they would capture her.

Then the pain would begin. She clutched the flower, bringing it to her chest to protect it, as if the flower might be afraid, too. She breathed in little panting breaths, trying to focus on the flower, but the pressure in her chest seemed to build. Her stomach boiled like she had just been given ipecac, but she didn't vomit. Her breathing seemed to come faster and faster and she couldn't control the acceleration.

Looking up, she searched the undercarriage of the truck for a place to crawl into. There was a small cranny she could fit into right there. Not knowing and not caring in that moment that, if the truck started up, she would die a horrible death, she reached up and climbed into a small gap. Dirty now, shaking hard, she waited.

The wait was long—or perhaps it wasn't. To her, it was as good as forever, and yet only an instant, at that. The terror too long, the reprieve too short. Mitch slid under the truck, wriggling in to give her a cold smile. "Come on out, little bitch, or I'll kill you."

He reached up and grabbed her ankle, yanking hard. She caught on the truck and her shoulder was wrenched from its socket, dislocated. She shrieked in pain, but still tried to kick and fight.

Swearing vengeance and cursing, Mitch moved in further, brutally twisting her arm out from where it was now helplessly lodged. With another agonized scream, she was yanked out, skin shaved off of her arm and blood flowing free. Her head battered against the truck on the way out, slamming brutally into the ground as she fell from her hiding place.

Forgotten, the pretty yellow flower tumbled free from her hand as she kicked and screamed, flailing around and scrabbling for freedom. Inevitably, inexorably, she was dragged into the cruel light of the sun.

Logger two had left, walking back to the main camp; one of a countless sea of faces who knew what was going to happen and walked away. A silent, endless phalanx represented in a single person. He went on with his life, perhaps once in a while thinking back on that moment. He left her there, minding his own business;

as that was the mantra of the time- mind your own business, don't interfere, it's not your problem. Besides, who knew what Mitch and his newfound compatriot would do if he bothered to try to save her? It was too dangerous to find out.

In his absence, the pair had their fun unimpeded by even a minimum of pretense towards morality or human dignity. It would be morally wrong to detail their actions, but if you're reading this, you surely know what happened. It was a savage attack with no concern for the size difference between an undersized child and two large men. The brutal rape that took place at that time was just one in countless others in those 4 years with the Joneses.

By the time it was over, there was blood, there was suffering, there was misery. She was raped such that what wasn't bleeding was just as sore as what was. Sandi was picked up by her less injured, not dislocated arm and thrown into the back of the truck in the storage area behind the bench seat like a piece of garbage after the shoulder was reset into its socket with brutal efficiency by Mitch despite the swelling. That shoulder would hurt for the rest of her life.

Since she had gotten dirty, she was 'washed' with a garden hose at the camp. Officially, to outsiders, she had fallen down a steep hill, of course. The Oregon mountains where Mitch was logging had plenty; and 'you know how retards can be'; so said Mitch. Everyone nodded in sympathy with the poor guy, and life went on as it always does.

CHAPTER 12
SQUALOR (DARREN)

DARREN HUNG UP the pay phone. The Jones house had burnt down just after he had finally convinced the Sheriff to start bothering himself with looking into Marie's disappearance. The 'investigation' this time, such as it was, had consisted of him showing up to chat up the oldest Jones foster son, Roy, pat him on the back, and leave. The first time, they had just asked Doris what happened and she had concocted some stupid story about their car going off the road. According to her, Marie got out of the car and jumped into a passing 'dark car' with a 'dirty man' and they had gone off together, never to be seen again. The previous sheriff had shrugged it off and said, "People like that run off. It ain't unusual."

Now, of course, the house had 'burnt down'. The investigation into that consisted of asking what happened and patting the Jones' foster kid who had 'inherited' it on the back. There was no way he was hiding evidence, right? Right? Of course not.

Irritation flared. The whole thing seemed so incredibly obvious to him. Here was a woman fighting to get her two kids back, and two days before she was to be given custody, she disappeared. To make matters better, two days before Mitch was to be served a warrant on an outstanding charge of raping one of the foster daughters, he had packed up and run off.

Now, the 'investigation' was nonexistent.

He knew what kind of reputation Marie had. She was a prostitute. During Darren's investigation, he had been told that she was prostituting the kids, also. In short, the two seemed to be fighting over who got to make money off of them. It seemed unlikely that it was true she was prostituting them, but he didn't know for sure.

What bothered him the most, though, was that nobody seemed to care. The Sheriff, even the previous one, simply shrugged. "She ain't hurtin' anybody, and we ain't got the resources to run around chasing down that sort of person. Jail ain't big enough, ya know?" How was prostituting your kids not hurting anyone, if it was true? Besides, the people saying that were related to Doris, and could easily have ulterior motives.

The Joneses, of course, were pillars of the community, just ask the frightened people around them. Especially so when the guns came out, which was anytime anyone so much as drove past the property on their way to somewhere else.

It didn't seem all that much different here. He thought he had found a place where the Joneses had stayed, but people were very closed mouthed. It was the way of things, of course. You kept your head low, did your job, and kept your mouth shut. Other people's lives weren't your business.

Since his business was quite the other way around, the decision to keep complete silence about anyone else's actions was definitely not working in his favor. Showing the photo around had done little, people turning away without even really looking at it.

He looked at his watch and swore as he realized he had forgotten to wind it again. This case was wreaking havoc in his life. He'd been on road trips and chased down felons and philandering husbands... but this case...he shook his head. He decided to just screw it all and head to the tavern at the end of the block. It was another place to ask around, and who knew, maybe a bit of liquor would loosen tongues.

Sitting down at the bar, he noticed that the clock on the wall said it was nearly 6 pm already. He had been asking around this hellhole dinky town for twelve hours. Ordering a whiskey, he let it sit for a few minutes. The guy beside him, stinking as if he'd been at it longer than Darren had been pounding the streets, leaned over and tapped the photo on the outside of his folder. "I know that asshole."

Two hours later, Darren had a picture of what had happened, and had something to go on. It was a thread, however thin, that connected the dots for him. The family was staying at various homeless shelters in each town they stopped in, eating at the soup kitchens... it was a migrant, nomadic lifestyle that allowed them to move large distances while staying relatively unnoticed. As he had suspected, Mitch was working manual labor jobs such as cherry picking, construction, and other forms of day labor. In this town, it had been roofing for a couple of weeks. Mitch had apparently worked for this fellow and taken off with a number of his heavier, more expensive electrical tools.

Bad luck for this guy; good luck for Darren. He was definitely on the right track. Weeks behind, but on the right track. He gathered up his folder and went to his car, forgetting to pay his tab. He rushed back in just as the bartender was coming out. They both laughed about it, and he left a generous tip.

His spirits high, he stopped at the gas station on the way to his hotel room. Heading towards the office to pay for the gas he had just pumped, a flier caught his eye. "Missing: Annie Hensman" He stopped to stare at it. The date caught his eye, it was 6 weeks ago. A slow frisson of discomfort crept down his spine. Annie had disappeared while Mitch and Doris were in this town.

He shook his head. He was making things up. Tilting windmills. It was a coincidence, it had to be—didn't it?

Little Annie's smiling face on the flier, her pigtail braids on each side clasped at the bottom by butterfly barrettes, would not let him sleep. He sat on the side of the motel bed, the scent of musty mildew all around him and permeating his clothes now that he'd been there so long, and stared at the floor.

The next day, he was in the 'rough part of town'. Little Annie, it turned out, was from the wrong side of the tracks. He stepped up to the front door of the old house, knocking and then pulling his hand away as cobwebs assaulted him from the side of the porch as a breeze wafted through. The scent of something long dead lingered and flies buzzed.

"What the fuck you want?" the voice came from the other side of the porch, and he turned to see a woman as old as dirt leaning on a cane much as he was doing. A smoke hung from her lip, its burning ash dropping to roll casually down the stained thing she wore. It might once have been a dress, he supposed.

"I was looking for Annie Hensman's family," he said.

"She ain't here. Took off, for all we know."

"I understand she disappeared. I wondered if I could talk to her family," he tried once more, firmer this time, and moving towards her around the decaying posts of what remained of the fence that had supplied the porch with a banister at some point.

"Only got Charlie left, and he ain't gonna talk to you."

"Who's Charlie?" Darren gritted his teeth. The woman was obtuse, to say the least.

"Her pappy—well, close enough. He her step-daddy. Her mom overdosed a few years ago, ain't never known who her real daddy is. Law won't let us get rid of 'er." She stopped, as if realizing she had said something terrible. "Don't get me wrong, now. We didn't do nothin' to 'er. She just a bad kid. Runs off all the time."

Her defensiveness made the hair on the back of Darren's neck rise, prickling with warnings he wasn't sure he understood. He raised his hands, spreading them wide, opening the right one and loosening his grip on the cane with the other one.

"I know you did your best to take care of an ungrateful little bitch," he said, hating the words even as he said them. To build rapport, he would need to sully himself with this woman's way of viewing the situation.

She nodded, relaxing. "Damned right we did. Fed her, put clothes on her back. Gave her every'thin."

He made small talk with her, hating her more by the moment. She waddled slowly towards the back of the house as they talked, and finally he asked the question he'd most wanted answered. "Did you happen to see this man around the neighborhood around the time she disappeared?" He held out the picture of Mitch.

She looked at it, squinting. "Hmm, might be, only if he had a beard. Can't be sure. Sorry."

As the door closed behind her, his heart sank. He was no closer to an answer, except that he knew for sure that this girl fit the type that Mitch and Doris liked to "take in". She was unwanted, which was enough for Doris. Any child no one else would take, Doris called her "Street Kids" and would take home.

In all his investigations, he had learned that at one point, the household had been 17 kids. Now there were 4. No one knew what had happened to 10 of them. Nobody cared, either. This couple was extremely careful in which kids they 'took on'. Kids nobody missed. Kids nobody wanted. Kids nobody would notice or ask about if they were gone one day.

Someone had missed little Annie, just enough to make a few fliers and report her missing. He would go to the police station and find out who. Once there, he learned that the school had reported her missing after being unable to contact the 'father'. The person who had posted the fliers turned out to be a teacher, who had felt guilty because the poor little girl seemed so alone in the world.

In the weeks that had followed her disappearance, there had been no investigation. "Kids run off. You would, too, if you lived with those people."

The problem he faced was that he couldn't argue with them. He likely would take off, anybody would, except that 'those people' were all Annie had in the world and she didn't know how to survive without them. If she had just run off, she would have ended up either at home or with a friend—and she had none.

Hating the necessity, but believing in his heart that it was already too late for little Annie, Darren moved on. There were too many stories in the world, too much hard luck. He had been paid to do this particular job, and his heart was heavy as he forced himself to turn his back on another statistic and carry on. It felt wrong, but he was, in his own way, alone in this, too.

His dad had warned him of this. He'd said plainly that you'll want to save them all. "You can't, son. You just can't."

Darren was sure he couldn't save Annie, but he was going to save James and Sandi, and Maureen and Ronnie. He was going to stop these two predators. He steeled himself as he closed up the hotel room and resumed his journey after turning in the key.

He was too far behind to waste another day chasing someone he believed was probably dead already or possibly with the Joneses. He left a part of himself in that town that day, though. Some bit of optimism, some fragment of hope. Little Annie Hensman had already been through so much. He forced his mind away from the likely gruesome manner of her final hours.

Everything in him screamed and shouted that Mitch had to be stopped. The predator in him, the hunter, the primal force inside roared to life and turned his focus towards the open road. His prey was waiting. He could also wait. Wait, watch, search… and one day, pounce.

CHAPTER 13
A BUBBLE BATH- OF SORTS (SANDI)

IT WAS BATH time. Sandi hated bath time. It was inevitable, of course, that she would infuriate Doris. This time, they were living in a small house out in the woods while Mitch logged. The house had a wood-burning stove and an actual bathtub. Everyone slept in one room, and the walls had holes she could look out of at night while the others slept. She liked this house... but bath time here was as bad as it had ever been.

This time, she was sore and tired and her back ached abominably. With her scoliosis, her back hurt all the time—but didn't everyone's? Sometimes it hurt worse than others, and today was one of those days. When it hurt too badly, it would sometimes cramp up and she wouldn't be able to get up if she lay down. Doris usually fixed that by yanking her up by the hair.

Cold baths could also make her back lock up with pain, and that was why she feared them in part. She stepped into the cold water—she always got the water at the end when everyone else was done—and shivered in the cold air. Here in the mountains, the nights were usually cold.

Doris handed her a washcloth, gray and stained and running with brownish-gray water. "Clean yourself up."

Taking the cloth, Sandi's hand shook so hard she could barely hold onto the cloth, but she rubbed herself as fast as she could. The faster she was clean, the faster she'd be out of this horrible cold tub. She'd had another "accidental fall" that day. She didn't notice the bruises and scrapes except when the cloth scrubbed cruelly at them.

Doris's hand suddenly yanked Sandi's legs apart. Staring between her legs, she snarled, in a cold, rage-filled voice, "Why are you red between your legs?"

Sandi fought hard not to tell her. She knew what would happen. Doris raged and punched her. Already beaten, her back screaming for mercy, Sandi finally blurted the truth. Mitch had done things to her there.

"You lying bitch!" Doris screamed. Her fury broke free like a raging river, and she yanked Sandi by the hair, shoving her under the water. Pulling her up, she screamed again, this time, "You seduced my husband, you whore? You little Jezebel?"

Storming out of the house, Doris was back moments later with a large cooler. The ice water from the cooler, with its remaining ice, joined the frigid, dirty water in the tub. Grabbing Sandi, who was now frantically trying to get out of the slippery tub, she reached around and gripped her by the neck before shoving her under the water.

All Sandi could see was Doris's furious face, screaming unintelligibly at her, and the bobbing ice. Pain and cold and terror made her claw and rake and kick. For an instant, she was above water, drawing great gasps of air, then she was under again, choking and convulsing, struggling for life.

Again and again, above the water, below the water. Already weakened, starving and shivering, she still fought. Nature had equipped her with self-preservation so that she could not cease fighting and trying to live.

As she fought to stay alive, for an instant, just an instant, the world slowed. Everything closed in on her, but as she began to lose the strength to fight, the world narrowed. A bobbing cube of ice caught her gaze and her eyes held onto it. Time slowed and distorted, and she saw the glitter of firelight on the ice cube. It sent diadems of rainbows into the coursing waves of the water, the light refracting, gleaming, incredibly beautiful.

Just for that second, for that precious, beautiful second that seemed to last forever, all she saw was that distant pinprick of light where the piece of ice danced, perfectly clear and sharp despite seeming so far away. There was an instant of peace, and of inevitability, and of acceptance. Momentarily everything else faded away, distorted as if happening outside of the real her. Eternity passed as everything was suspended.

For all that it felt eternal, it was also gone in an instant. The fractal of time, breaking up and coming apart and slowing as it had, instantly returned to the savagery of reality and Doris's hate-filled face once more took dominance. Sandi was ashamed, because she had felt elated. She had been about to die, but she was yanked out of the water, gasping in a bit of air with the water that she coughed and spat into Doris's twisted, wrathful face.

Spittle flew from the screaming tyrant and mixed with water and tears on her face before Sandi was plunged once more into the abyss of the bathtub where there was only cold and dark and terror. For all the horrors the tub represented, Sandi had gotten off easy for 'seducing' Mitch this time. Usually, it was much, much worse.

CHAPTER 14
SHARING IS CARING (DARREN)

"IT WAS THIS guy?" Darren waved the photo again, wanting to be sure.

The logger nodded, his eyes skittering away again immediately. Cigarette smoke lazed into Darren's face as the logger took another long drag and let it go in a slow, steady stream. "It was him." He flicked the cigarette butt negligently. "He's a putz, always thinking he's owed something, if you catch my drift." He picked up his jacket and slung it over his shoulder. "And that kid of his that he dragged with him every day is all kinds of fucked up. Dude can't handle her and shouldn't have her."

Darren leaned back against the Mustang, rubbing his forehead. He was only a couple days behind the pair now. He had caught up fast once he knew they were staying in homeless shelters and sometimes halfway houses when Mitch would pull a pity party about being a drunk.

The thing with Mitch and Doris were that they made no friends anywhere they went. People remembered folks who thought they were better than everyone else and who were meaner than snakes.

The nature of the pair made them easier to follow than people who could blend in.

Interestingly enough, as well, Sandi's disability also made them stand out. Her reactions were often violent and people either remembered her with pity or with anger. The very thing that made her an easy victim made her memorable.

He pulled out two other photos. One was the one of Marie, Jimmy, James, and Sandi. The other was of a totally different family. His face oddly drawn and angry, the logger pointed to Sandi without a moment of hesitation. "That ain't them, but that's the kid alright." He meant that Marie and Jimmy weren't with them—which of course, Darren knew already.

"Thank you," Darren said. He passed the logger a 20 and climbed in the Mustang as the man wandered towards the nearby flop house. Having been undercover in the DEA, Darren had no problem blending into places like this. He knew how to talk to people, and nobody ever pegged him for a 'pig', even now. He had the bearing of a predator, but not the general demeanor of a cop. That time, all too brief, doing something he had loved, stood him in good stead now.

He looked at the photo and the two kids in it. Then he looked at the photo of Mitch. A cold rage burned in him. This guy was going to pay. Dropping the folder on his seat, he headed out, allowing himself to enjoy the sense of elation and hope. The Mustang's engine rumbled satisfyingly under him as he turned onto a paved road and it shot forward, wanting to run, wanting the chase as badly as he did.

Two days later, though, frustration had set in. Mitch and Doris hadn't headed further up into Oregon as he had expected. Set back two days and too much gas money, he returned home before heading inland from Oregon into the states.

By this time, school had begun, and it was that which gave him his next real break. He stopped at a gas station again. One thing that people traveling across the country always needed was fuel. They couldn't avoid the gas stations; and most towns only had one or two.

"Oh, that's Joanne. She was in my class a few weeks ago." The woman behind him in line had poked her head around him trying to look at the picture. He obligingly held it out for her to look at more closely. "Poor thing. Wouldn't sit at a desk no matter what we tried." The woman's look didn't match her words. Kind words, said with distaste on her face.

"Oh?" It was a short word. All it said was, 'Do go on, I'm listening.' That single word had garnered him information in almost every situation. He knew many secrets because he simply asked that one inquiring word and didn't give any appearance of judging the response.

People opened up when they felt heard.

"Her mother is a real piece of work. Dragged her out of school in front of everyone when she had to come get her for behavioral issues." She sighed, her face now turning soft, matching her words, "I just let the poor thing sit in the back of the class on the ground after that. As long as she had paper and crayons, she was happy."

The teacher's pained eyes met his. "Why are you asking about them?"

Darren decided to tell her, "They're on the run, and those aren't her real parents."

The response was electric. By the time the woman was finished telling him how "sweet little Joanne" came in with bruises, welts, and burns, Darren was exhausted. Joanne was the name the Joneses had changed Sandi's to, and there were times when it was uncomfortable to try to discuss it with people in a way that made sense, with the two different names.

He had also realized that Louis, the teacher, had been angry at Doris, not Sandi. He had tried to ever-so-casually ask if Louis had turned the Joneses in to Child Protective Services. She had nodded abruptly. "They don't do anything. They never do anything. About as useful as tits on a turtle, pardon my language, if you will." He smiled and made a face to indicate he 'hadn't even noticed, honest.'

Yet the same theme rose over and over again. Sandi and the other kids were only in school because the shelters required children to go.

It was a grace that she was old enough to go now, he knew. The stories along the way of how she had been treated while "in the field" with Mitch—and who knew why that was going on—were pretty horrifying. At first he had thought they were exaggerations, but the more time went by, the more chilling it became.

He stopped for the night at yet another cheap motel. It stunk of cigarettes, mildew, and old socks. He dared not think of what else might be contained in the general malaise that underlay the too-strong scent of air freshener tablets.

He sat at the card table that squatted beneath the dingy curtains and counted his cash. The hopeful feeling was fading fast. Head in his hands, he sat in the chair, the sound of crunching metal and the feel of gravel grinding into his flesh crawling into his mind again.

Trying to forget the haunting images, he turned his thoughts to the four kids he was hoping to save. He picked up the folders he had carefully put together. Every kid he could find that the Joneses had "taken in" were kids nobody wanted. The foster system was overburdened by American Indians. Ronnie, being one with a birth defect that made him bowlegged had been nearly sent to a boy's correction facility despite having no prior history of criminal activity.

Maureen was black, adopted not long after birth. Like Ronnie, there was little information to be found. Where had she come from? "The court" had given her to the Joneses... and the same went for Maureen. Yet there were no local records of what court. With Maureen, the records were sealed because she was officially adopted; the only one official in any way. The rest of the kids had no documentation that he had been able to find.

It wasn't hard to get kids into school. While it was 1977 and the world was more modern now, there were some things that just hadn't caught up yet. Nobody checked documents for kids going to school —why would they need to? Darren was of the personal opinion that it wasn't modern as much as naive. Then again, doing what he did, he was much more aware of the horrible things in the world than most.

One valuable lesson he had learned; people protected their ignorance with the same zealousness as they protected their peculiar, deviant religious notions or their favorite sports teams. The need to be right was as powerful as the need to eat for some people—and if someone suggested they might be wrong, eating often became optional for the duration of the argument.

He stretched and prowled the room, the cane slowing him down. He finally settled on the bed, pretending to himself that the sheets and comforter were probably clean—no, really—and got out a book. Living the job was mandatory while on the hunt, but he could do his best to create an oasis during it.

Predictably, it didn't work. At length, he lay back on the bed, staring at the ceiling. Time crawled while he told himself it would be okay, he was closing in, it was going to work out. As the night ticked away, he finally couldn't stand it any longer and left the motel room, leaving the precious Mustang in the parking lot and walking to the bar several blocks away.

Inside, he met a pretty girl with long black hair that had flowers in it. They walked back to his hotel. Once there, she pulled out China White—heroin--and offered it to him. After his stint in the DEA and seeing what drugs did to destroy lives, he threw her out after she became insistent that he join her. She could have all she wanted, but he could have all he wanted, too; which happened to be none.

Unable to sleep, unable to work off the restlessness that drove at him relentlessly, he lay on the bed and watched the clock numbers tick over, tumbling one after another in a restless fall until wan light exposed the streaks of what he hoped had been cleanser on the card table.

His constant, uncomplaining companions, the cane and the Mustang both said nothing as he left the hotel at the first whip crack of dawn. He couldn't sleep while the claws of certainty were buried deep into his mind. Time was running out for those kids. He knew it in his very marrow.

CHAPTER 15
PORK 'N BEANS! (SANDI)

IT WAS THEIR second day in this gas station. It was on the corner down the street, and Sandi and James walked with Ronnie down to the corner each day so he could get smokes. This day, Sandi squatted behind the bread rack. She watched Ronnie carefully as he chatted with a girl. He being a young teen, talking to girls his age had begun to become something worth doing. He was chatting up the girl and the owner of the store, who was working the cash register.

While he was occupied, Sandi very carefully opened one loaf of bread. She took a single slice of bread, dropped it on the floor, and then stuffed it inside her shirt, smashing it against herself so it wouldn't be visible. The flattened slice of bread was pushed into her waistband to keep it for later consumption when she would not get caught.

Looking up again, hyper-focused on Ronnie's position and activities, she returned to her work, opening another loaf and taking just one slice. Each slice was carefully dropped, smashed, and hidden.

That was when it happened. She looked up and met the eyes of the store proprietor. In that moment, she knew only terror. She'd gotten caught. She knew only that she would be punished, they would move again, and she would suffer horribly for it.

He turned away, a strange look on his face. Sandi could not know or understand that look in that moment. She had no basis for knowing or understanding compassion. She had no knowledge of kindness. The look was incomprehensible to her, and it wrought only fear for her right then.

It was only in the years to come that she was able to examine the face in memory and see it for what it was. The man knew she was starving. He knew she was terrified. He could do nothing to help her from a legal standpoint but call upon an overburdened and uncaring "Child Protective Services" or call the police.

He looked upon the face of privation, misery, and starvation with no recourse at all.

Many would do nothing. He chose a different path.

The next day, when Sandi arrived and headed for the bread—for she had gotten away with it, and was too hungry not to try again—he left Ronnie occupied at the front desk again and put a sandwhich on his desk in the office of the store. The desk was in full sight of the bread aisle.

Unfortunately, what he did not understand was that Sandi couldn't eat anything that hadn't been on the floor. Food on the desk was human food. She ignored his sandwich that day.

How he figured it out may never be known, but he began to place the food on the floor. There were delights such as Sandi had never known—or at least could not remember. Macaroni and cheese! Peanut butter and JAM on bread! Jam, can you imagine?! Her favorite, though, was pork and beans, though it presented an unusual problem because it was messy, and of course, she didn't know how to use a spoon.

For all of that, each and every new food was a feast of kings. No longer did she steal bread, but rather she "stole" the man's food that he so carelessly, stupidly dropped on the floor. Silly human!

Pork and beans-- the feast of kings, not for its flavor but for the kindness which provided it.

CHAPTER 16
MANY MEMORIES OF MIDNIGHT (SANDI)

THE WINDOW was cool against her face, the street lights overhead ticking by one after the other. She watched their golden glow, absorbing herself in it, losing herself in total focus on that one thing. Like a metronome, the lights ticked by one after the other.

Eventually, too long elapsed before another. Moments ticked by and no glow. Her eyes turned up to the ceiling of the world, endless darkness with infinitesimal lights that offered the world no illumination. She did not wonder what they were. She did not count, for she was not able.

She merely watched, disoriented yet fascinated as the car and the world moved on and on and on while the stars remained with her, synchronized, forever beside her however far she traveled.

She knew what would happen this night, as it had on so many other nights. Beside her, she heard the soft sobbing of the boy. He would scream before the night was over. She knew this. She would scream, too, if they could force it out of her. She had learned that the screaming made things worse; more violent, more horrifying. And the laughter… they would laugh if she screamed. They would laugh when he screamed.

The new ones didn't know not to scream.

Lights began ticking away again. The car slowed. Time accelerated and she tried to stop it by pretending she couldn't feel the rough hands that seized her and dragged her out of the car. She pretended not to notice the boy and how he begged.

The begging was worse than the screaming. He'd learn. They'd teach him. She had tried to whisper to him, but like everyone else he couldn't understand her. She had tried to warn him. She had tried to help him. Instead, her heart throbbed with dread.

This time it was a house. Ever since they had left home, it had been houses. At home it had been a church, but now… now it was houses. It was arranged differently, but the basics were the same. The small tub dominated the middle of the room, sitting on a black-shrouded table. Heavy music played and people shouted over it, their faces covered in black. Every time they laughed, the sound was sharp and cruel, cutting into her mind like the tiny point of a stiletto dagger.

Laughter. They always laughed. The greater the pain, the louder their laughter. It was true all the time, not only during these times, but these 'events' were especially cruel and brutal.

They talked amongst themselves as Sandi and the boy were tied to the bottom of the crude, fabricated crucifix. At whatever signal specified the beginning, Sandi was dragged to the golden-colored basin in the middle. Heavy and sturdy, it didn't even rock as she was shoved into it, fighting silently the entire way.

The heavy music throbbed and boomed as someone screamed into a microphone. The record skipped several times, sometimes repeating and sometimes silencing the screaming singer. Sandi fought hard, biting, clawing, jerking and twisting with all her pathetic strength. A fist to the side of her head made it ring, but did little to stop her abject denial of what was to come. "Not again, not again." It was the same thought again.

She fought in silence for no other reason than sheer, unmitigated defiance. She would not cry. She would not scream. Foremost in her mind was to never scream. Never, ever.

As always, the fight to avoid the basin ended. She was tied with cruel ropes that dug into her. Trapped.

Trapped with people's hands on her, their body parts on her... Men gathered around her, discarding the black they wore except for those covering their faces. They laughed, bumping into each other and talking excitedly.

They gathered close and, from Sandi's ignorant perspective, peed on her. Sandi had no concept of what was really happening, nor even understood that there were two different things that could happen with a man's penis.

Once this behavior tapered off, they began to rape her. The basin held her in such a way that her legs were roped apart. They raped her in every way, nearly killing her a number of times by strangulation. Her skin tore, and she tore inside, the pain mounting as she fought with all she had not to scream. Never, never scream. Both men and women were there; all who had any interest in doing so hurt her.

She was also burned, whipped, bitten, pinched in every area of her body until she existed in blood and pain and little else. She was ashtray or toy. Cigarettes or cigars were put out on her arms, already marked with scabs and scars of the same. Ongoing for years, most incidents did not leave scars. The ones that did were agonizing.

Behind her, out of her sight, the boy was chained, manacled to the peculiar crucifix shape and was being beaten and brutalized and raped as well. He screamed. She cried. They laughed. She tried not to hear him. She tried to ignore the sounds of skin beating against skin, barely heard above the harsh music.

The rapists laughed.

A fog of drugs began to fill the air, the scent horrifying and cloying with the smell of blood, sex, and body odor. Many of the people did not wash themselves, though Sandi only understood that they stunk. Some were old, some were not. Sometimes they were obese, sometimes they were gaunt. Women with weird, flat breasts. Men with bellies so big they nearly smothered her. Sometimes they were beautiful people, but most were extraordinary in their very ordinariness. Big, little, short, tall... They all laughed. Like cackling chickens, they laughed. The vast majority were men, but there were many women as well.

When the group was ready to move on to worse things—yes, worse things—Sandi was removed from the basin. The boy was placed there in her place, and she was dragged to the sofa to be fondled and raped by those waiting their turn at the boy.

For a brief time, most concentrated on the boy, pouring blood over him from a bucket to the accompaniment of laughter and cheers. They raped him in a line one after the other, talking and laughing as they waited. So organized, so courteous to each other. Such a facade of civility.

And the laughter got louder and more frequent, the women often screaming with it.

Then they turned to Sandi again. Too weak now to fight, she was forced to more sexual acts. They now wanted her to participate. When she refused, she was beaten brutally and raped anyway. By this time, she had come to a place where she refused to even try to pretend she enjoyed their attentions. Her refusal to pretend enjoyment roused them to rage. Her apathetic acceptance of being kicked, beaten, and otherwise abused was a source of immense frustration.

They wanted her to fake not merely compliance and exhaustion, but lust for their brutal abuses. They wanted her full participation. They wanted the illusion that she was a willing party to their infliction of pain, and she had learned that there was no difference for her if she did or didn't. Compliance did nothing for her.

They had also learned this; they began to beat the boy, untying him and dragging him over to lie in front of her. This... this could bend her to their will. Her own pain might bring indifference, but they could hurt someone else instead.

This time, for the first time, it was different for Sandi. She had failed to comply last time. Too exhausted, in too much pain, she hadn't the energy to force herself. She hadn't the heart anymore, either. When her mother had died, she had believed she would never be free.

This right here, she believed now, was forever. Her eyes met the boy's for an instant as cruel fingers closed over his throat.

In that moment of seeing his terror, of seeing his suffering, she understood. She realized fully and completely that this was his forever, too. The only hope she believed any of them had, had been her mother.

She fought back. She fought back this time, not unable to comply, but rather unwilling. She fought back and she watched him die and she chose. She chose that he would die and know no more suffering. No one else would ever whip him. No one would do what had just been done to them. For him, it would be over.

She chose, and as the boy died, she finally, at last, screamed as they kicked her, punched her, and whipped her again. She screamed because something inside her had broken again. Something ugly had taken root there.

When it was over and she lay in a pool of her own blood and vomit, and urine both hers and theirs, she stared into the boy's dead eyes. Eyes like her mother's had been... strange, unseeing eyes that did not respond to anything. She stared at him and she cried, regret already stealing her temporary courage.

Her limp body was assaulted again and again, and she tried to ignore it, staring into the boy's eyes. He was free. He felt no more pain. He would not scream anymore this night or any other. He would not learn to eat dog food on the floor.

She knew he would experience no more of the pain that, even in that moment, was ripping through her. Still, she wept for him, her heart screaming long after her throat would no longer release sound.

All around her, the music pounded and people laughed.

Some time later, she was dumped on the floor, discarded in the corner nearby the boy. An orange lava lamp slid greasily up and down in the confines of the glass that held the moving oils. Its light fell across the boy, making the blood glitter and glow in a path of its light. His dead eyes stared upwards, away from her, but she knew them well.

The distorted orange glow made the red blood look like it was moving and alive. Tears fell down Sandi's face as pain twisted inside her. She already regretted what she had done. She already hated herself for it. She cried for him. She cried for his pain. She cried from her shame. She watched the light slither and glitter and her tears dried as his blood dried, but she couldn't stop the pain that rose and fell inside her of her in waves. The voices around her, the cruel laughter, the grunts, the music, the slap of flesh against flesh was all grotesque and twisted to her.

She could not bear herself. She could not bear what she was, what she had done. Her heart cried out for the boy. A different sort of pain took her over. Her heartache swelled and rose until she thought she might die of that alone. She made a long, high sound over and over in her throat as she grieved.

Did they not understand that the boy was dead? Tears came and went, but the orange lava lamp continued its greasy slide up and down. The blood no longer glittered, now it was dull and lifeless. It had mostly dried. "I'm sorry," she whispered in her broken, useless voice. The party dragged on, the room was hot and the air stunk.

When it was over, she was dragged into the bathroom and shoved into a bathtub. Cold water sluiced over her and somehow she managed the energy to shiver violently. She was dumped in the back of the car again. This time, she stared at the stars alone, the greatest ache not that of her body, but that of her forfeited soul.

She was wrong to do what she did. She knew that. She had killed him. It was her fault.

She did it two more times until they caught on. Five lives total, three of whom she intentionally chose for instead of being unable to make herself pretend pleasure. They would never again hear laughter while they were torn inside.

She hated herself for what she had done. She hated herself more because she was jealous. Jealous that he was free, and she would never be. She was ashamed of herself, deeply ashamed of herself. The people in the room laughed while the boy lay there, dead. Her body burned with pain, but the deepest pain was inside her. Shame ate away at the fabric of her very soul, devouring her heart with bleakness.

At another 'party', she lay in her own refuse: blood, vomit, feces, urine. Every inch of her hurt tremendously. All she wanted was to die. She cried out to God again, begging and pleading that she be allowed to die. God did not hear. God did not care. She was alone in a world full of people who laughed at her pain and her beloved Jesus did nothing. Jesus didn't love dumb animals, anyway. She knew that. She didn't deserve it anyway. She had murdered someone. She truly was evil, and she knew it now.

However it *should* have made her feel, it left her with a black pit of pain and was its own torture for decades to follow. She would listen to the words of others and their 'savage' deeds, keeping her secret... she had killed by deliberate, calculated inaction.

She would awake in the night, trying not to scream. She would rock herself for hours in the darkness, terrified of sleep, terrified of the memory of the kids who died. Boys she killed through inaction. Sleep would be elusive for decades, the hours of the clock ticking away as she tried to avoid the memories and the pain and the knowledge of what she had done.

You see, she was the monster now.

CHAPTER 17
MISSING AND IGNORED (DARREN)

DE LEANED back against the brick wall, listening to the guys around him shooting the breeze. He was watching and listening carefully, adding appropriately to the conversation when asked. These were tough men. They worked a hard, blue-collar job and they looked upon their masculinity with pride. He knew their type, but he needed to get a bead on their specific group dynamics.

After a while, he knew which one of them to approach. When 'Dice' walked away from the group, Darren waited a while and then followed. Dice stood smoking, the cig curling wisps of gray up into the night air.

"Yo," he greeted simply.

Darren just nodded, stretching a bit as if relaxing now that he was away from the group. He waited, forcing himself to the patience he had learned from his training and his work undercover.

"Nice night," Dice finally commented casually.

"Sure," Darren agreed easily.

Dice looked at him shrewdly. "You ain't tokin'," he observed passively, meaning Darren wasn't partaking of the marijuana being passed around.

Darren gazed back out into the night. "You ain't tokin' neither."

Dice chuckled. "No, I ain't. Don't nobody trust a negro when the drugs come out, boss."

Darren had picked that up in Dice; he wanted to get ahead and yet he needed to appear groovy at the same time. "I did a stint in the DEA. I seen what drugs do to folks. I ain't havin' no part of that."

They stood in silence for a time. "Why'd ya quit?"

"Didn't quit, my man. Couldn't do it no more." He held up the cane. "Still got the heart for it, but don't matter if I ain't got the ability." He spoke in as close to the language the group had used as he could, building necessary rapport.

"So what you doin' now?" Dice tossed the butt of the cig into the night air, the still-glowing ember at the end falling away and bouncing heedlessly on the concrete, red sparks dancing in the darkness.

"I got myself a gig doin' some private investigative work."

"Ahh, that's why you hangin' over here with the negro, then, eh? Think I'm most likely to rat everyone out?"

Darren met his eyes now. "I can't say I understand what you're goin' through, my man, but I know people. I'm tryin' to save some kids. I think you're the kind of man that's gonna matter to."

Dice's face relaxed. "Kids? Damn. Fuck, I hate people who mess with kids."

"It's this dude here." Darren handed him the photo of Mitch.

Dice sneered. "That asshole. He a racist piece of shit. He got that little black girl he draggin' around everywhere. She wouldn't sit still for her ma to brush her hair, so he done pulled that little girl over and shaved her head with a strop razor, right at the wash-trough."

He referred to a trough of cold water kept at the front of the shop, where the guys could clean the worst of the mud from the farm off before entering their barracks. The water there could be refreshed by pulling a chain and running more, but the water was chilly, coming as it did from an underground cistern.

Dice continued, "You don't do that, man. That little girl gotta live with that bald head for months. It's one thing if she wants that cut, ya know? She didn't, though. Fought hard. Good pair of lungs on that little 'un. Fucker laughed about it, too. Cut her several times, didn't give a fuck. Do you think he'd shave that little blond kid's hair? No. Hell, no. It's only cause that girl's a negro he fucking shaved her head. What you need from me?"

"You gave me most of what I needed. I needed to know if they'd been here. That's what matters most. I gotta git them kids away from him."

"Yo, what you bastards groovin' on over here?" Another voice joined them.

"Nothin' man. Just shootin' the shit. Talkin' 'bout visitin' Benny's for a cold one."

Darren took Dice's lead and carefully didn't ask the newcomer about the kids or Mitch, surreptitiously sliding the photo into an interior pocket of his lightweight windbreaker jacket. He went with them to the bar, having a drink before making his way back to his motel room.

Another town, another stinking motel room, too much money gone and not enough available. He lay back and considered what Dice had said. Mitch had been there. He had abused one of the kids right in front of everyone. It was the same story in every town. Different halfway house or shelter, different day... but the same story.

He sat up suddenly as a question dragged at him. It had been hiding in the back of his mind for the last few towns, but now it coalesced with startling clarity. The same story in every town... the abuse... neglect...

And missing kids.

His heart seemed to skip a beat and he had to dial his adrenaline back a notch. Was there a kid missing from here, too? Was there more to the repeating pattern than just the abuses?

Darren knew something was terribly wrong, but this realization made his blood run cold. His research into the Joneses told him that they'd had something of a revolving door at their house. Kids, mostly with disabilities, would come to their house, and then simply not be there later. Kids of various races would arrive, the kids who couldn't find good foster homes like black kids, American Indian kids, Mexican, or handicapped kids.

Doris called them her 'street kids' and proudly announced that she took in the kids nobody wanted. But if nobody else wanted them, where did they go? Nothing in the records said anything about them being taken away. The Sheriff had nothing about the family except incidents of poaching, arguments with neighbors, and the typical things associated with poor country folk with nothing better to do than fight.

He got up and made his way slowly to peer out the window, simply wanting to feel less restrained. Where were all those kids? The trail of missing kids, it dawned on him, didn't start when they went on the run.

The cold feeling of dread that had been pursuing him the entire time he'd been on this chase caught up to him, slamming into him with full force. These people were worse than sinister... they were coldly evil and monstrous.

Sleep eluded him, as it had seemed to do regularly on this trip. The night ticked by with excruciating slowness until he went to eat 'continental breakfast' of rice cereal in a bright paper bowl decorated with Snoopy and Charlie Brown.

Then, he waited in crazed agony until a reasonable time to approach the local police. Folder in hand, he slowly made his way up the very long stairway up to the doors. In pain already, he pushed his way inside, requesting to speak to a duty officer.

The next hour was one of the most excruciating of his life. He carefully explained who he was, then explained what he was doing. He asked if any kids went missing and when.

The cop sitting across from him shrugged. "Not too sure. Think some negro went missing a few days ago. Prolly just a runaway, though. You know how them people are."

Darren pinched the bridge of his nose. He wanted to take the man to task, but knew that it wasn't the time or the place. Rage burned in him, Dice's words haunting him with their incisive understanding of the world. The complacency ate at him as much as the blatant racism. In this day and age, people should know better; it was 1977, for fuck's sake. But no, of course not.

"What day did she disappear on?" He settled for the question, seething impotently at the uncaring attitude sitting in front of him.

"A boy," the cop said, putting his feet up on his desk. "Dunno what day."

Darren ground his teeth. "Can you look at the report?"

"Didn't take no report."

Darren sat and stared until the man dropped his feet off of the desk and protested, "Was just a runaway negro kid, man. If we took a report every time some negro ran off, we'd be swimmin' in reports. It's just the way things is."

Darren hated this guy. He hated him so much he actually, to his surprise, found an urge for physical violence rising inside him.

Trying to focus on what was most important to his case, he pulled the photos out. "Any reports on any of these folks?" he asked the cop, trying to speak to his level.

When he had been talking at Dice's level, it had felt like fitting in with a friend. Speaking at his man's level was more like talking to a pile of mud and trying to make himself understood. He wondered idly if this cop realized he was ten times dumber than Dice, who had a lower education level and was forced to live segregated, not to mention the racism he faced every day.

"Yep. That one broke up Denny's a bit." He pointed at Mitch. "Got in a fight with some other 'necker." He was referring to roughnecks, men who most often worked on oil rigs, but would take other jobs if they needed to.

Darren asked more questions, but again, a report had not been filed. After all, 'those people' were just like that. They came and they went and why write a report when you'd never see them again?

"Be worse for them kids without no dad, 's the way I figure it," was the way he excused not arresting Mitch.

Maybe that was true in some cases, but Darren was convinced it wasn't true here—not at all. Or at least, not with Mitch as the 'dad' in question, anyway.

He left, standing at the top of the immense stairs and sighing heavily. He would be burning with pain by the time he got down. Sucking it up like a proper buttercup, he set out for the sidewalk below even as the stairs seemed to stretch and grow longer with every step like a bad trip.

Everywhere he turned, it was racists, assholes, and putzes. No rest for the weary.

The next day, weary and bleary-eyed, he returned to speak again with Dice. Their rapport remained from the previous encounter, and soon Dice was telling Darren the entire story of the missing kid. He had Downs Syndrome, Dice explained.

CHAPTER 18
KEEPING HER PLACE (SANDI)

SANDI WAS squatting under the table in the soup kitchen. She had learned that having something over her head prevented people from easily and unexpectedly grabbing her by the hair. Flimsy as the safety was, it afforded her some, and she took anything she could get.

She watched warily around her, leaning forward over her knees to ease the never-ending fire in her back. Unbeknownst to anyone, she had mild scoliosis, a birth defect resulting in a curvature of the spine. Whilst hers was mild, it rubbed on a nerve and caused such tremendous pain that at times her back would seize from it, spasms branching out so brutally that she could not overcome the powerful muscles enough to sit up or even roll over for however long it took for her to calm the spasms enough to move.

For this moment, though, she knew only that fire, savage and painful, seemed to live perpetually in her back. The squatting position eased the burn slightly—the best she could ever get. The position, however, had a trade-off. She was vulnerable when she couldn't see, and so she soon abandoned the stance and looked up again, watching... watching... always watching.

Danger was all around her all the time.

Beside her, a stranger's German Shepard dog lay sprawled. It was unconcerned with her, as she was with it. Generally, she shared space with dogs easily and frequently. Had she known how different this time would be, she might have chosen a different table, but she took a tiny measure of comfort from the beast's presence.

As the people began to move around, she inched closer to the wall behind her, its cold concrete pressing against her aching back. The fire was burning hotter than usual this day, the ache deeper, the misery complete.

"Here, bitch," Mitch said, shoving her bowl of food—dog food—under the table towards her.

A voice gasped in outrage, "You call her 'bitch'?" and older woman's voice demanded.

"Won't answer to anything else," Mitch said, his growling voice warning her to silence.

She said nothing more, though she made an audible huffing noise.

Sandi inched towards the food, then caught the bowl with a finger and dragged it to her, hugging it against her chest between her knees. It was as she lifted the first bite of food towards her mouth that it happened...

The dog, having sat up at the appearance of the dog food, lunged at her. In a short, brutal burst of violence, it ripped into her face with a snarling bark. The teeth refused to release her face as she, in silence, tried to scramble away from it. Dog food went flying as she fought back to the best of her ability. The dog's tooth had penetrated into her eye socket, only by good fortune pushing her eyeball back instead of piercing it. Its bottom jaw had closed on the bottom of her cheekbone, deeply piercing the skin.

In the next instant, the table was yanked up and back so that it slammed against the wall, sliding down between her back and the wall as the top of the table crashed against the wall with great force.

The raging fires in her back screamed in protest, roaring into an inferno. The dog shook her wildly, responding in its own way to the unexpectedly violent removal of the table from above. Sandi kicked the bowl again, sending more food flying.

Mitch yelled. The other patrons of the food kitchen screamed or ran for cover. The owner of the dog seized its collar and tried to drag it away, forcing its jaws open. Finally pulling the dog back, the owner tried to pull it further away, but Mitch caught him and punched him, bellowing in outrage.

Released from the dog, Sandi scrambled to get as much food into her mouth as she could.

Released from its owner's hold, the dog scrambled to get as much food into its mouth as it could, too, then realized it had competition. It clamped onto Sandi's hand, snarling in an angry frenzy.

With her other hand, Sandi desperately grabbed more food, stuffing it into her mouth, the food now mixing with the blood that poured copiously down her face. Trying to keep the dog away from her food, desperately hungry, she scrambled, too weak to resist as the dog inevitably pulled her away.

Screams echoed around her, shouting people scuffled. Sandi grabbed for nuggets of dog food.

The dog lost interest as it noticed that some human food had fallen from the thrown table. Sandi ignored the human food and grabbed more dog food, dodging between the legs of the people. Her torn hand was stepped on as she grabbed for food and she nearly cried out—but not quite. When the person lifted their foot with an apology, she stuffed the precious morsel in her mouth, bloody and dirty as it was.

A kind face appeared in front of her, and for only an instant, Sandi dared the unthinkable and met a real person's gaze. She instantly looked away and looked for more food, ignoring the person in hopes of one more bite.

Pain, as present as air, throbbed through her, and at last, overcome by the hunger and the misery of her body, she curled into a ball and sobbed as quietly as she could. She was so hungry, so very hungry. She wished, not for the first or last time, that she could just die. She needed to just die already and not feel so hungry, not hurt so much.

Someone touched her and she almost shrieked in terror. She scrambled away, tried to find a place to hide, tried to find freedom... and failed. Pain and terror mingled together in a confusing jumble as voices babbled and people crowded in... she had no idea how she would be punished this time, but it would be really, really bad. She had been really, really bad and she would pay for it.

Seeing a table that was unoccupied in the other room, she bolted for it, dodging hands and legs and crawling under it, beating at the hands that tried to pull her out from her refuge, biting, clawing, hissing... terrified.

The fear beat at her, the pain hammered at her, and people grabbed at her, crowded her, said pretty words to lure her out so they could beat her. Cornered with no hope in sight, she did the only thing left to her.. she paradoxically fought for the life she didn't want at all.

oOoOo

Sandi crawled into the large drain pipe that ran under the road. The large concrete tube made a perfect hiding spot for someone of her size. As she settled herself inside the entrance, she heard a sound from behind her.

Whirling, she found a puppy lying there staring at her, whining. It dropped its head onto its paws, eyes staring at her with a sweet, innocent look that she found difficult to resist. However, a previous incident with a dog biting her in the face had made her wary of them, and she sat staring at it for a very long time.

Slowly, details of the poor creature's plight began to make themselves understood. Something had mangled its hind legs badly. It was also painfully thin, probably starving. It was trying to inch towards her with its front legs, whining in its desire to be close to her.

Scared of it, she squatted in long silence, too afraid to touch it and too afraid to leave. Some time later, it drew near her, and she couldn't take it another moment. The stalemate inside her finally shifted and she reached out gently to caress its tiny head.

It licked at her fingers in clear joy, bumping at her to pet it when she stopped. She crept closer to it, petting it and wishing she could fix it.

Doris's voice calling her name made her bolt from the drain, terrified that they'd find the small, pathetic creature. That night, at dinner, she didn't eat her food, rather stuffing it into her pockets. Wary as she always was, she caught a man watching her. He smiled, and she shivered. Trying to throw him off, afraid she would be punished, she ate a kibble. He turned away as one of the men he was with captured his attention.

After dinner, she crept out to the drain pipe. The puppy licked her again, and she dropped the food in front of it. The puppy couldn't get the kibbles up off of the ground, as he couldn't twist his head enough to get a grip on them. She fed him the kibbles one by one, his sharp teeth hurting her fingers as he scarfed them desperately.

Leaving only at the last moment, she hurried to bring him her morning kibbles the next day. She had tried to be extra, extra good to earn some. He left some, so she ate what he had not, her stomach pinching with ravening, painful hunger.

It became her routine. The puppy was tiny, but still she fed him first, then sat with his head on her lap. She wasn't even aware that she was actually sitting to allow him to place his head there. She petted him tenderly for hours at a time, sometimes crying because his mangled legs looked so painful and sore. She told him stories, and he didn't even care about her inability to speak properly, looking up at her with perked ears as she whispered tall tales.

It was a cool, bright day when disaster struck. She was petting him when Ronnie's head appeared in the entrance to the drain. She jumped in front of the puppy, but he had already seen it. He called out and Mitch came to see, as well.

Mitch dragged her out of the drain by the foot even as she tried to escape into it. Dragged along the concrete, she was bleeding by the time he got her out. The puppy, the sweet, sweet puppy, was growling and barking in fear and anger.

She was thrown down and the puppy yanked out, yelping and crying in pain. She jumped and cried, trying to reach him. Mitch, laughing, held it aloft out of her reach. "You want your puppy back?" he asked.

She stopped, backing away and shaking her head.

His eyes narrowed. "Yeah you do. You want this puppy back." He said to Ronnie, "The little bitch had a puppy." They laughed.

He dangled the puppy, yanking him away as she reached for him.

He handed it to Ronnie after they grew bored with their game of keep-away. "What do we do with unwanted animals, Ronnie?"

Ronnie sighed. "You have to put 'em down."

"That's right. You have to put 'em down. Don't need no extra mouths to feed. But you gotta do it like a man. You gotta make it cry a little, because it needs to know who's boss. You gotta make sure all the little bitches know who's boss, too. They see you making the other dogs whine, they'll respect you more, right, boy?"

"Yeah, Dad," Ronnie agreed, looking anywhere but at them. "Yeah, you gotta show them who's boss."

"So show the little shit who's boss, kid."

Ronnie, as trapped as Sandi, began to beat the puppy with a stick.

The puppy's cries destroyed Sandi. She squatted, afraid to cry, afraid to let out the screams and pain inside her. It would only be worse. It would make them laugh. The poor, sweet puppy. It wasn't the first time Sandi had gotten an innocent animal killed by wanting it to love her. She tried so hard to be silent, to not let them know that she felt like she was dying inside.

But they laughed anyway as the puppy cried. They laughed as

the puppy looked at her, and she couldn't save him. They laughed as she looked away, because they knew she couldn't close out the sound of the puppy's screams.

When they grew bored, Mitch threw it into the storm drain and handed Ronnie a large stone. He hit it over and over.

They left, leaving the shattered puppy in the drain.

Sandi slowly crawled inside, her heart aching. The puppy's head was distorted, blood and brains coming out of one side of it. She squatted beside it and petted the only part of the body not bloody. She rocked back and forth, keening. The pain was so immense inside her that it couldn't come out. It would never come out.

The sweet puppy. The sweet puppy had died grotesquely because of her. He lay still and she couldn't stop touching him. She finally took the last bit of food out of her pockets. She had learned he sometimes got hungry later and she'd started keeping it, just in case.

Now, she took the kibbles and placed them beside his mangled head. She started to crawl from the drain, but hunger pangs hit her hard again. She stared at the food, picked up one kibble and raised it to her mouth. Tears came again, and, deeply ashamed without knowing why, she put it back down beside him and scurried from the drain. Seeing one of the bright, beautiful yellow flowers she so loved beside the drain, she picked it and placed it beside his head and then backed out again.

She stopped to look back as she headed towards the car and saw the man from a few days ago standing by some trees nearby. He was watching her quietly, his face solemn. For a reason she didn't understand, it almost made her cry again. She ran before she could.

CHAPTER 19
UNEXPECTED ALLY
(DARREN)

DARREN STOPPED at a small gas station on the outskirts of the rustic Midwestern town. It smelled of oil and gasoline and greasy hotdogs. The dogs made his stomach twitch with hunger. He'd been driving all day, stopping only for nature's call and fuel.

Heavy clouds and still air hung all around him. The clouds promised rain, and rumbled with the fury of thunder. Gold spikes of light flashed and the clouds grumbled their discontent. The sky glowered as the evening darkened, the clouds reaching down with grotesque blobs of threatening downpours.

The store loomed in the darkness, the lights vainly attempting to illuminate the area. The Mustang sat at the pump, protesting the silencing of her engine with a glowering sheen as a light flickered overhead, its ballast dying a slow, painful death.

Frustration rode him, the talons of a furious vulture. He glanced down at the eagle's head of his hated cane; the symbol of his losses. "See what you got us into?" he asked it. The eagle ignored him, glaring forward from hooded eyes.

"Yeah. Nothing to say as usual." He snorted and finished

pumping his fuel. He headed inside to pay, worried about his meager remaining funds. He was far enough from home that he had just enough to get him back, and no more. He couldn't even get to a bank, as his franchise didn't extend this far.

He went inside and got one of the hotdogs and a cola. Taking it to the counter, he pulled the photos out more from habit than hope this time.

"Hey man," the owner greeted him, his face friendly, but disinterested.

"Thanks," Darren said after he paid the guy. He pushed the photos towards him. "Happen to have seen any of these people?" he asked, not interested in the typical 'no' anymore.

"Yeah. Yeah, I seen them. They stopped in here often." The man no longer looked friendly. In fact, he looked cold, distant, and wary. "Friends of yours?"

Darren fought to tamp down the surge of hope that tried to break free. "No." He pushed the photos again. "You sure it was them?"

"Yeah, man. I'm sure. Like I said, they came in a few times a day. Kid had a crush on my daughter." He pointed at Ronnie unerringly. "Came to buy smokes, and talk. Whole lotta talking."

His face was still hard, though. Darren's statement that he wasn't friends hadn't warmed him in the least.

"Anything else you can tell me about them?" Darren stopped him, instead, though, realizing he was letting his eagerness get ahead of him. "Wait. Let me explain." He pointed at James and Sandi. "These two kids?" When the man nodded, Darren continued, "Their mom disappeared. When the Sheriff went to serve a warrant on Mitch," he pointed him out, "they took off. I want to get those kids back and get them with their grandparents. I don't believe they're safe with those people. Not at all."

The thaw was immediate and total, but it didn't return to friendly. The man's hand reached out and he touched Sandi's picture in the photograph. "Her. She...." His voice trailed away, and Darren realized he was choked up with emotion. He got himself under control with effort. "She's starving. She was stealing bread from me."

Darren bristled, expecting the man to start in about retards and the like.

"I felt so sorry for her. Sweet little thing, terrified of everyone. I left food in the back room for her." His sigh was heavy, heartfelt.

He looked at Darren then. "It took me too long to figure out she'll only eat off of the ground. I gave her all kinds of things kids should have, you know? Mac 'n cheese. Pork 'n beans. Wieners. Stuff kids like. I watched her a few times while she ate. She didn't even know how to use a spoon."

Darren could tell that, for whatever reason, that last seemed deeply disturbing to the shopkeeper. He said nothing, waiting. He found that people often wanted to talk, once they had begun. He was not to be disappointed.

"I called Child Protective Services on them. I guess they went out and talked to the parents, and they said she wouldn't eat anything except dogfood. I know that's not true, but they wouldn't listen to me. Even told me that if I pestered them again about some retard who wouldn't eat like a normal person, they'd charge me with harassment." He sighed heavily again, his eyes filling with unshed tears. "They took off immediately that night."

He looked up at Darren. "I couldn't help her. I couldn't help any of them." His voice had tightened and lowered, pain leaking into it like ice spreading over a lake in winter.

A thought occurred to Darren, and he decided to test his theory. "How many of them were there, if you don't mind me asking?"

The man shrugged. "Just the four kids and the parents that I ever saw clearly, but I swear I heard another kid in the back of that camper they're driving."

Darren thanked him and pushed a twenty towards him. It was the least he could do to know he was on the right path. The shopkeeper pushed it back. "Just help those kids."

Darren pocketed it and turned to go, before turning back slightly, "How long ago did they leave?"

The man shrugged. "Not last night, the night before. Wasn't long."

Darren's heart pounded hard. He was closing in. The gap was narrowing fast and he could barely control the boiling sense of triumph. Just when he had feared they had evaded him, he was actually gaining on them.

He would have bolted out the door, but for the blasted cane. He settled for hobbling fast. Sort of fast. Hardly the stuff of heroes, but it got him into the Mustang.

The big car roared to life at the turn of the key, humming peacefully. Darren stomped on the accelerator, and with a bellow of surprise, the Mustang threw off her fetters and leaped from the parking lot of the gas station. Roaring with the sheer joy of freedom, she blasted onto the open road just as a crash of thunder and a fork of lightning slammed into the ground beyond the building, lighting up the darkness in stunning, shocking clarity for a moment.

The Mustang hurtled along the road into the darkness of the encroaching night. Behind her, baleful at the escape of its morsel, the sky opened up and a torrential explosion of hail and rain fell to the ground, chasing the vanishing car in vain.

Without Darren's restraint, the car left all pretense of civilization behind and opened up her mighty engine, her headlamps beaming into the night before her like harbingers of some long-forgotten dragon. Her throaty roar reached out into the night, causing nocturnal creatures to turn and look... and cower.

CHAPTER 20
THE BOY (SANDI)

SANDI CREPT closer to the boy on the chain. The new ones were always on a chain at first if they tried to escape. The boy had tried to escape several times, and now he yanked incessantly on the chain. He had cried at first, and fought. Now he lay on his side, his face streaked with pale dirt that stood out starkly against his dark skin.

She had learned a long time ago to be careful. Once, she had released Kevin from the chains in his bedroom. He had beaten her with an electrical cord for her trouble. She had broken the rules and done something wrong, so she deserved it, yet she had felt betrayed none-the-less.

Now, she tried to be very careful as she slowly inched towards him, needing to stay just outside of his reach, but close enough to drop the kibbles where he could get them. Wary as ever, she watched everywhere, ensuring that no one else could see her.

She took one more crabbing sort of scuffle towards him, dropping the small handful of kibbles she'd hoarded when no one was looking. Instantly, she jumped away, hiding behind a tree and watching him. He remained where he had been, rocking back and forth and weeping. She crept back slowly, picking up the kibbles, watching him to make sure he didn't come after her.

Painfully slowly, she worked her way nearer to him, clutching the dirty kibbles in her hand. When closer to him, she dropped them and fled. Her focus, never the best, soon wandered, the kibbles forgotten.

Several hours later when they were found, she was beaten.

She realized that he wasn't going to eat, and she stopped trying. She did, however, creep out that night to sing to him. She loved to sing, and she thought it might soothe him. It soothed her to try to soothe him, and made her feel strange things that she didn't understand, but which she liked. Chained to the back of the car as he was, he was also given nothing but some rags to sleep on, just like her.

What she did wasn't really singing as much as it was a sort of open-mouthed humming, but she knew no different. She didn't know how to make the words go with the humming, so she made up words and hummed them. She had sung to Kevin for a while, but after he beat her, she had stopped. She wouldn't know why he'd done it until decades later—he'd been forced to it by Doris.

Sandi was so used to sleeping on a hard floor with nothing but rags that she didn't even need the rags anymore. They often worsened the ache in her back by putting lumps in places that threw it out of alignment and increased the intolerable misery.

She crept closer to the chained boy as he cried, afraid to go to him. He would hurt her, she was certain. If he didn't hurt her, he would get killed for her helping him, or she would. Feelings she didn't understand rose in her and struggled to express themselves. These feelings were painful. His sobs bothered her, twisting inside her as if they were her own. She had no words for things like empathy, compassion, or remorse but she could still feel the pain of them.

Eventually, she crept away, curling up on the rags she slept on and listening for any signs of danger. She dozed here and there, but with her acute hearing, the weeping from the boy would not release her to sleep. When finally morning arrived, it was to Doris dragging her forcefully from her bed by the hair because her back would not relax enough to allow her to get up on her own. The scoliosis radiated pain out into her back, making the muscles there lock up so hard with spasms that she wasn't able to unbend it.

She didn't mean to be lazy, she really didn't. She couldn't help it, because she was a bad person, a terrible sinner. She was born even more evil than most. Doris made sure she remembered that she was, too, as she beat her, then strangled her. Come hell or high water, Doris promised, she would beat the evil out of Sandi if it killed her to do the deed. Doris made it clear that hurting Sandi hurt her, too, and Sandi shouldn't make her do these things. All she had to do was obey, but she was evil and Doris had a responsibility, no matter how much it hurt her, to beat the literal hell out of her kids.

She seemed to forget at these times that Sandi was a dumb animal who had no chance of going to heaven, anyway. Not even Jesus loved her, only Doris did. Only Doris.

Sandi struggled to her feet to obey as she was commanded to help gather their things for the trip into town for Mitch's work. Every day, the camp had to be broken, because they weren't allowed to be where they were.

Every muscle in her body protesting, she carried as much as she could. She was always eager to help, desperate to please. She tried to drag a heavily laden bag towards the truck, and a punch to the side of her head sent her sprawling. She hadn't been paying enough attention, in her desire to please and not get hit... she usually could have dodged that blow.

Warily, she went for something else, not even certain who had hit her. Arms trembling with fatigue, hunger, and pain, she took another grocery bag of clothes, barely able to lift it, and headed for the truck. Having been bad and given her food away, she did not eat that morning, and had not eaten the night before. After all, if she could give her food away, she obviously didn't need it herself.

She sat on their belongings on the floor as the truck bounced up the dirt road towards town. Every jolt blazed down her aching back, but she remained silent. The boy was also silent now, and eventually fell asleep, falling onto her and trapping her, putting her leg to sleep.

She dared not react, knowing punishment would be swift and brutal. She was surrounded and would not dare to draw any attention to herself. The pain increased as the load shifted and something dug painfully into one of her bruises, battering over and over with each pothole.

She dared not rest, she dared not move. Time crept by slowly, the heat of the camper becoming unbearable, despite the one available window being open. The small breeze it afforded did not reach her on the floor.

When they arrived in town, she again could not make herself walk as her leg, deprived too long of circulation, protested and did not hold her weight. She was slammed back into the camper, told to stay there or die, and the family left, only she and the boy remaining in the truck. He soon slept again. She did not, though she was exhausted.

Like the pain in her back, it was just another sensation that she had to deal with. Sleep was dangerous because it made a person unaware. Even now, the boy slept, unaware that the family was returning and, if they couldn't get into the truck around him, they would beat him.

She argued with herself and decided not to try to wake him. Every time she helped someone, she paid the price. Something unhappy came, and guilt arrived with it. She was a very bad person. She always had been, she always would be. She was a dirty, worthless sinner and clearly deserved even worse than she got.

A tear trickled down her face and she poked the boy. Twice. He stirred and she tried to tell him to move, but he began crying and wouldn't respond. She was beaten for making the boy cry, because clearly, she was the only reason he had to cry.

She hid under the truck for the entire rest of the day when they stopped, hurting too much to play. By evening, her arm was swollen and she ate her kibbles with the other hand. Unpacking for the evening was torture, her body protesting on every level. There were things to be done and she had to help. She struggled under the burden of the small parcels she was given to carry in silence. Complaint would do nothing but enrage someone, and she'd hurt worse by the time they were done with her.

CHAPTER 21
BURIAL WITHOUT FANFARE (DARREN)

DARREN WAS LATE again, but this time, he had missed them by barely a day. They had stopped to sleep, and Darren hadn't. He asked among the rough migrant workers, and they spoke little outside of the fact that the family had been there.

It wasn't until late afternoon, when frustration had begun to settle in, that he got the break he needed.

"You lookin for them Jones people?"

He turned to look at the man standing a ways away from him, shifting from foot to foot; ready to bolt at the slightest hint of provocation.

"Yeah," Darren agreed, "I'm wanting to save those kids." He didn't ordinarily open with that, but he was going to lose this guy if he didn't.

The guy didn't relax. "The girl, she found a puppy. She was feeding it. All she gets is dog food." He took a step back.

"I know, it ain't right. I ain't a cop, y'know. And I'm not gonna say nothing' to nobody."

Now the man relaxed slightly as Darren deepened his faux accent to make himself more relatable to the other man. He did whatever it took to build rapport. It was the difference between getting or losing his tip. He had said many a sickening thing when he was undercover. This was little different.

It took one to know one... he had to be like them to learn from them. When in Arkansas, do as the Arkansans do, as the saying went-ish.

"How you gonna save her, then?" The guy was young, maybe 20 or so, and terrified still. His disbelief colored his voice; he trusted neither cops nor strangers.

"I'm a private detective, man. Them kids was kidnapped. Their family is payin' me to help save them."

All the fight left the fellow. Money was something he understood. He didn't trust people who pretended to care about others, but he did understand the universal pressure of money.

"She found a puppy, and they tortured it and killed it to make fun of 'er. She was feedin' it her food. I don't know where they went, I'm real sorry."

The puppy story was eating at at the guy. Darren wondered why. He chose his usual method and let the boy talk. Silence was the greatest inducer of talking in others that he knew of. Better than questions, because questions often gave you only the answers you thought you wanted, when you even got an answer.

"They tortured it. Threw it back and forth and laughed at her. I didn't help either of them."

Darren understood the nature of the man's problem then. He hadn't stepped up and he couldn't live with himself. The fact that he probably would have gotten himself beaten senseless if he had tried didn't play any part in his concept of himself as a failure, either, except perhaps to make it that much worse.

"It's still there."

Darren blinked at the suddenly blurted statement. "What's that?"

"The puppy. I wanted to bury it, but I..." The guy looked around nervously.

"Can you show me where?" Darren asked. He pulled out some mentholated petroleum jelly and rubbed it under and slightly into his nose, then offered it to the other man, "It'll mask the smell."

The guy, barely more than a kid, took some and led Darren down a hill that he struggled to navigate with his cane. The smell already overcame him despite his precautions. The young guy pointed at a round storm drain, his arm over his nose.

Darren slowly maneuvered around the many piles of construction equipment and supplies to get to it. He understood immediately why the guy had wanted him to see it. The puppy had old wounds on its hind end, it had obviously been badly injured and had crawled into the drain for safety.

The rest of the damage was new, though, and it was brutal. This puppy had suffered before it died, and all he could hope was that the poor thing went quickly when it was finally allowed peace. The poor creature looked grotesque, and Darren pushed back a sense of revulsion. He had seen death, he had even seen suffering; somehow, this was different, more horrible, more stark in a way he couldn't explain.

He looked around and saw a shovel that had been left propped against the side of a pile of pylons. He found some loose ground, the best he would be able to do, and opened up a small, but deep grave. Still using the shovel, he went back to the puppy and scooped it up. As he was about to turn away, he saw them.

Small pebbles that at first appeared to rocks were actually dogfood kibbles. A limp dandelion lay in their midst. A tremor passed up his back, and his eyes burned. This was all so dreadfully wrong. He went back to the hole he'd dug and placed the corpse in the grave, then stood staring blankly. He was physically exhausted. The walk down the hill and then the shoveling had left his leg in tremendous pain. Getting the puppy and returning it without the cane had added to the burn.

He looked back at the concrete tube where the puppy's last

supper lay discarded. That it had survived this long without being scavenged was a miracle. It couldn't last. Painfully, slowly, he moved back to the drain and pushed soggy dogfood onto the shovel with a stick.

He knew it wouldn't matter to anyone. No one would know. No one would judge him if he didn't do it. The forlorn kibbles gathered together on the shovel, huddling in a small pile in a dent.

Nobody would know but him. He wasn't going to let the kid down on this. She left those kibbles for that puppy, and Darren was going to see that they made their way to the grave with it. The puppy, if it had given her even a moment's love, deserved it.

The small pellets fell into the hole when he finally reached it. Then ever so slowly, he filled in the hole, knowing that if he stopped now, he might not find energy for it later. He probably shouldn't have done any of this, but it was impossible for him not to.

He finished and sat down for a long time. His mind churned with the enormity of it all. He needed help, but it was just him. He had no one here to turn to. Anyone else who came would take too long. He was road-weary, physically weary, and heartsick. He looked down and saw a bright yellow dandelion bobbing its little head at him. They were rare in the fall. Remembering the one with the kibble, he picked this one and lay it across the fresh turned earth with a tender pat.

He looked at the long embankment he would have to climb, and finally made himself just get up and do it. He would get stiffer, not better. This day's work would put him behind because it had exhausted him. He looked once more at the puppy's burial mound.

Yes, it was time to get back to the chase, time to fight the good fight. In 5 minutes, because god, was he exhausted.

CHAPTER 22
INTO DARKNESS AGAIN (SANDI)

ANOTHER DARK night, dragged from bed, warned to silence. It never occurred to her to cry out to anyone for help. She wasn't all that smart, but she wasn't stupid enough to risk that. If Mitch was dragging her out of the house and into the truck again, it was because she did something wrong.

She huddled in the camper, watching the world go by outside. It was dark, but objects loomed from the world, darker still. Black trees whisked past, shadowed against a black sky. Now and then, houses would speed past, bright lights where people lived lives that Sandi didn't even think to wonder about.

The boy cowered in a corner, thumping his head against the side of the camper. Sandi rocked back and forth, trying to ease the pain in her back, despite the knowledge that far worse pain was coming. The boy was going with her and she wanted to sing to him, because soon he would scream.

Soon, she would try not to scream, but it would happen anyway. They always made it happen. She wasn't strong enough to stand up to them. She hated herself for it. She hated that she was so bad and worthless. She wished she would die tonight. She was scared, but she didn't cry or beg anymore. She didn't hope for anything but for it to be over and to be dead.

But life wasn't kind, and she arrived. It was a strange house again. The boy screamed and screamed until he died because they couldn't take his 'wailing' any longer. They tossed her into the corner eventually, her body alight with terrible agony. She lay beside the boy, relieved and yet sad at the same time that she couldn't see his eyes to be sure he was really free, for real.

She had stopped crying and screaming hours ago, but she dared not rest, she dared not sleep... she was ever alert, ever afraid. She sang to the boy after a while, sobbing softly, her voice completely drowned out by the music and shouting of the people as they talked to each other. Even if he were alive, he couldn't hear her. But she was sorry. She was so, so very sorry.

Unexpectedly, for whatever reason, they remembered her and she was dragged by a leg out into the room and the nightmare resumed. She soon found that despite the hoarseness of her throat, she really could scream again.

CHAPTER 23
DONE AWAY WITH (DARREN)

"NO, MAN, no kids have disappeared." The cop was curt. "We're a small town here. Kids disappear around here, and we notice."

He started to turn away, then cocked his head. "Did find some dead queer out on the highway a few days ago, though."

Darren's irritation level spiked. Whatever a person's view of such things, it didn't belong in public and it didn't belong in police work. A cop had to be impartial because his job was too important. Not wanting to get into it, he turned to go.

"A queer kid. Not local."

That stopped him in his tracks. "What?"

"A negro, not from these parts." This time, the cop started to turn away.

"Was he autopsied?" Darren needed to know.

"Yeah. Old man Marshall checked him out. Was just some queer kid, probably killed in the way those perverts like to get off. You know," he made a strangling motion at his own neck, a disgusted look on his face.

"How old was the kid?"

The cop shrugged. "Thirteen? Fourteen? Not really sure."

"Thanks." Darren hurried out of the station to his car.

He immediately went to the nearest restaurant. In small towns like this, it was the best place to find out the things he wanted to know. Soon, he had a full belly and knew where to find "Old man Marshall", the local family doctor-slash-coroner.

A bell tinkled as he entered the doctor's office. An elderly, wizened man looked up from the desk.

"What can I do ya fer, young feller?" he asked amiably.

"I'm curious about that kid found out on the highway," Darren informed him, then sat back to wait.

"The faggot?" Marshall blinked over his glasses at Darren. "What do you want to know about him?"

Darren cringed. "Mind if I ask what his injuries were?"

The man frowned. "What for?"

Darren explained that he was hunting pedophiles who had kidnapped some kids, and was wondering if this kid was one of their victims. Marshall seemed to consider, then dug through a filing cabinet and handed him a folder. "Can read it over there," he pointed at another desk, littered with paper.

"Actually, do you mind if I take some copies?" Darren asked, since he really didn't want to sit here. He didn't like this guy at all.

"Sure, buddy." The coroner was casual in his disinterest. Darren knew the coroner would be far less likely to accept his request if the deceased person in question was a local or wasn't 'a faggot'. It grated at him, but pointing out the egregious error would not help him in his present circumstances.

Thanking him courteously, he left angry, making his way up two flights to the parking lot. Back at his hotel, he sat down and looked at the notes. What little there was, was very sparse. Race: Negroid; Height, weight, eye and hair color; then notes of the damage. John Doe had extensive anal tearing due to sodomy, his genitals had been mutilated (specifics weren't noted), he had multiple contusions from being beaten, and he had died of asphyxiation caused by strangulation. Cause of death was noted, however, as auto-erotic strangulation.

To Darren's shock, horror, and dismay, the kid had been cremated that very day, upon permission from the DA, who felt there was no sense wasting time or resources on a case of sexual misconduct by unknown homos gone astray.

The report was incredibly short, the autopsy based upon a theory accepted as fact rather than a theory being based on the discovered facts. Darren looked up at the cane. "Well, this is incomplete. Guess we're headed back."

Sighing, he gathered the paper up and went back to the coroner's office. When asked if the kid had downs syndrome, Marshall snorted. "Niggers don't get that, kid."

Darren stood stock-still. He very slowly, very carefully said, "There is a black kid missing from the last town I stopped in, along the path of these people I'm pursuing. He was officially diagnosed with downs."

Marshall snorted. "I'm telling you, kid, niggers don't get that."

Darren was convinced that the problem was that this man didn't really care what medical issues a black person might have and wanted nothing more than to just tell them all to go jump in the ocean and not come back.

"What happened to the body?"

"Cremated it. Don't have room in the cemetery for a faggot's corpse." He said it with obvious relish, having caught on to Darren's 'nigger-loving' attitude.

The only thing that moment that stopped Darren from punching the man in the face was the knowledge that the living children he was trying to save couldn't afford for Darren to cool his heels in jail for assault.

"You're a piece of shit," Darren told him.

"You're a nigger-lovin' faggot," the old man replied. "Get out and don't come back."

Darren didn't plan on it. He stalked out to the best of his ability, shaking with fury. In a modern society, attitudes like that shouldn't exist. The fact that they remained commonplace, even in those in authoritarian positions ate at his soul.

"Son, you can't fix everything. You have to pick your fight, commit to it, and give it everything you've got. There will always be distractions. If you spread yourself to too many causes, you'll fail them all." His father's words were scant comfort as he tried to keep the prize in mind. He had children to save and the world was full of evil.

It was hard to walk away and it filled his heart with lead.

Back at the hotel room, he picked up the phone.

"FBI, this is Angie Monahan, how may I direct your call?"

"Hello, Angie, my name is Darren Burr. I'm pursuing criminals who have kidnapped some kids and are on the run across the country. I need some help."

"One moment, sir, while I direct your call." The switchboard clicked and Darren heard ringing again.

"This is Rich," a voice answered.

"Hi Rich, my name's Darren. I'm a PI investigating a case of a missing woman. Her two kids have been taken on the run across the US by foster parents--"

"Do the foster parents have legal custody of the kids still?"

"That's unknown, there's no documentation of that--"

"But they're foster parents?"

"Yes, so I'm told, but there's no documentation--"

Rich sounded bored and annoyed now. "If they're foster parents, and the woman is missing, they're best off where they are. We don't get involved in these kinds of cases."

Darren ground his teeth in frustration. "There's a warrant for his arrest in Idaho on charges of raping one of the foster girls--"

"That's an allegation of sexual conduct with his own child?"

"She's not his child--" Darren almost threw the phone receiver as the man interrupted him yet again.

"That's still a matter that we don't deal with. We don't have the manpower to investigate every person who's accused of sex abuse."

Darren's frustration level spiked. "Listen, everywhere I go following these people, kids are disappearing. I was in a town a few days ago where a kid with downs went missing. I arrived here, and they had found a kid murdered on the highway near town."

"Was it the same kid?"

"I don't know," Darren wished he did, as the guy was finally showing some interest. "They cremated the body."

"Why would they cremate a murder victim?" Rich's voice rose in outrage.

"The kid was raped and strangled. He's a black kid, so the racist coroner didn't care about him."

It was a bad sign when the reply took a few heartbeats. "And you don't even know it was the same kid for sure?" Rich's voice had changed to irritation, the interest and outrage vanished like dew in a forest fire.

Darren's heart fell. "No, the coroner doesn't believe black people can get downs syndrome, and--"

"Well, if the coroner says the kid didn't have downs, it's not your kid, is it. This is not the kind of thing we can waste time and resources on, sir." He hung up without even a courteous 'screw off, asshole'.

Darren slammed the phone down with more force than it required. Fury, outrage, and frustration boiled in him. He grabbed his cane so he could pace the room, then slammed his fist against a door frame, careful not to harm either fist or frame. "FUCK!" he swore, "fuck, fuck, fuck!" He needed help badly.

None was to be forthcoming. The FBI didn't care. The cops and the coroner were firmly against him, and his quarry was proving remarkably elusive. He looked over at the folder on the bed... and kids were dying. He closed his eyes and despair blackened his mood.

He opened the folder again. No photos, nothing. He ran his hand down the page, whispering softly, "I'm sorry." Dice wouldn't even get to know what had happened. Darren had no proof, but there was no doubt in him at all that this kid was the one from Dice's neighborhood; the kid that everybody took care of because he needed them. The kid forgotten and ignored by police in two different towns.

He looked over at the photos of the kids he was trying to save. Would that be their fate?

A tremor wracked his body. No. He wouldn't let that happen.

"Sometimes, Darren, life just sucks. Sometimes really shitty things happen to really good people. Life doesn't give anyone what they deserve, it's impartial. Don't live in the fantasy that people get what they deserve in life; they don't." Father's words, father's wisdom...

'Not this time, Dad,' Darren thought to himself. 'Not this time. I'm never giving up.'

Yet he felt like it. To his shame and regret, he felt like giving up. This was turning out to be harder than he ever imagined. He wasn't sure he could do it, especially not alone.

Life, he knew, was not kind. It was impartial, like the sun. The sun sent its light down for everyone; life sent shit down for whomever it landed on.

He sat down and the cane's eagle head stared at him. He stared back. "What?" he said. "I didn't say I was quitting."

The cane glowered at him in silence. He sighed. "Yeah, not this time. Life's a bitch, but that doesn't mean she always gets to win."

The cane didn't reply, of course. It just sat in silent censure of his lack of faith. He turned away, not wanting its condemnation of his insidious, depressed thoughts. He kept trying to psych himself up into believing he could really do it. He would get up and go, and just keep going. Pick your fight, never give up.

He sighed and tried to sleep.

CHAPTER 24
AFTERPARTY (SANDI)

MORNING CAME upon Sandi as she slept, and the first creeping light of dawn warned her. She tried to get up, her back screaming a protest. Her entire body crawled with agony, and she tried desperately to overcome it and get up. She had to get up!

These mornings were especially dangerous to her, because these were the days when Doris would beat her worst of all if she didn't get herself up. She groaned and moved slowly, her body protesting every breath she took. She was always more sore the couple days later than the day right after one of Mitch's 'parties'.

Finally able to move herself, she crept across the floor towards the door out to the outhouse bathroom. It was so cold that her feet felt numb, and she was clumsy. She got into the outhouse, but her fingers, hands painfully bruised from the previous night, wouldn't function right.

She peed herself in her urgent need and inability to function. Immediate terror set in, and she curled up in the corner of the outhouse, her body shaking with pain and cold and fear. There was no way she could go inside, so she hid, shivering and crying.

Doris found her, of course. She dragged her in for a bath in the cold water remaining from everyone else's baths. Nobody wanted to carry more water in to heat up for the stupid retard, after all. Doris began yanking her clothes off, stopping suddenly.

"What's this? Why are you red here again?"

Sandi refused to tell. She wouldn't even say that Mitch touched her when Doris began to strangle her. Stopping finally, Doris dragged Sandi towards the tub, threatening to drown her if she didn't tell her how it happened.

Sandi tried to explain, to save herself, but Doris knew it was Mitch... and she hated Sandi for it. Jealousy spawned and Sandi had to pay for seducing Mitch. Doris would see to it.

"You little fucking whore. You think you're going to seduce my husband? You think you're going to steal him from me? You think you're so fancy with your blond hair, don't you? Little miss perfect, all prancing about and waggling your hips, trying to draw him away from me. Let's see how sexy you are now."

Grabbing a handful of hair, Doris pulled Sandi towards the stove in the livingroom. There, a curling iron waited, sitting in the coals of the wood-burning stove. While most of the time, Doris used an electrical curling iron for this job, this house had no electricity. This time, the curling iron she used was an old model that was heated on the stove.

Sandi fought and screamed with all her might, but Doris had little problem subduing her. Not only was she weakened already by her ordeal, but she was also starving and emaciated. She had no strength with which to fight.

Doris pinned her down on a low stool by the simple expedience of practically sitting on her. Once pinned, she moved clothing out of the way and shoved the curling iron inside Sandi's already abused and torn body. Pain ripped through her, and her shrieks took on an unholy volume. Torn flesh was burned savagely, the burning relentless and brutal. The entire time, Doris ranted about seducing her husband and how Jesus would send Sandi to hell for what she had done. The curling iron was just a taste of what the demons would do to her. Sandi was going to hell because nobody, not even Jesus could love her.

Every part of her screaming in agony, Sandi still fought a fruitless fight as Doris put the curling iron back in the stove. When it had reheated sufficiently, she shoved it into the other entrance, brutally uncaring at the screams from literal burning pain searing torn flesh once more.

When it was over, after what seemed hours, Sandi was forced into a nearly freezing bath, the water far and away too cold for comfort, but not quite cold enough to provide relief and numbness. When that was over, she was put to work, dragged into the cherry orchard to pick cherries with the family, barely able to walk. This night, she had not gotten off easy. Doris liked this punishment, but the need to reheat the curling iron in between had made it worse in a way.

Later that night, Mitch beat Doris. The children huddled together in terror as the fight raged around the house.

The next day, while Sandi, barely able to move and still in extreme pain, once more picked cherries, Doris wailed to the other women on their team about how Mitch had beaten her so badly that she had miscarried. The women there picking cherries also gathered around her, comforting her as she informed them that she just knew the baby had been a boy, and that she loved him so much. Her poor baby boy, gone in the night... It was her eighth miscarriage, she sobbed. So many of her babies dead. So many...

Hours of weeping and sobbing later, they went to their erstwhile home.

The next day, Sandi was informed that she had to go to school, or they would have to leave again. Having no real idea what that meant, and wanting only to feel better, she nodded that she understood and yes, she could act like 'a real person' at school. She would do anything to please and not get beaten again—if she could only figure out what that actually meant she had to do.

CHAPTER 25
ON THE DOLE (DARREN)

"DAD, I'M NOT kidding. He cremated the body the very day he did the autopsy. Immediately."

His father ranted on the other end of the phone, saying everything Darren felt, and most of it better than Darren could have.

"I did call the FBI, Dad. They hung up on me. Since the body was cremated, I have no proof it was the boy who disappeared a few towns ago, and the fact that immediate cremation was completely unethical doesn't seem to bother them at all. How local coroners and prosecuting attorneys handle cases is up to them."

The phone crackled slightly as his dad responded. "Did you explain that he has an outstanding warrant?"

"I tried everything I could think of. They don't care."

Silence reigned on the other end for a time. "Son, sometimes you have to know when to let things go."

Darren closed his eyes against the pain that rose in his heart. If even his dad thought it was impossible, who did he have? "I can't, Dad. Not yet. And I need you to wire me some money overnight. The payment ran out and I am nearly at the end of what I had on me, too-_"

"You said yourself that no one will help you, Darren. You gotta cut your losses. Come on home." His father's voice was sympathetic, but firm.

"I can't. I don't have enough money to come home." He kept going before his dad could respond, "I'm close to them. I'm really close. And Dad, some really horrible things are going on here, I know there are. Worse than we thought or had been told. Kids disappear from wherever they go--"

His father was surprisingly patient as Darren went on, laying the situation out in full. "I'll send enough for a week, and the trip home. Nothing more."

"It's my money; I'll be paying it back as soon as I get home."

"A week, Darren. I won't rescue you again. You gotta let this go. You can't win them all. There's one of you, there are endless cases. Spread yourself too thin and you end up helping no one."

Darren ended the conversation as soon as courtesy allowed, disappointed and disillusioned. He might catch up to them in a week. It was possible. He was close now. He worked hard not to let the demon of disappointment overcome him.

He sat drearily on the edge of the bed. Looking up, he found the cane once more staring at him with accusing eyes. "What're you looking at, putz?"

The cane did not venture a response.

The wire transfer didn't come through until the next day at noon. Darren set out immediately. He had no help and only a week. He glanced at the cane again. He wanted to be back in time before the motorcycle accident. He wanted to be undercover. He had always felt like he could accomplish something there.

Now, he felt like he absolutely had to accomplish this, but would certainly fail. "Thanks for nothing," he told the symbol of his unwanted life change. Sighing, he decided he'd been on the road too damned long when he started talking to inanimate objects and half wishing they'd respond. 'No, Darren, you don't have to do this. We'll just go back in time and undo that unfortunate series of events. Someone else will do this.'

But no one else would. It was Darren or nobody.

Poor kids. They were so fucked.

CHAPTER 26
WE MEET AGAIN...
(DARREN AND SANDI)

SANDI WAS NOT able to act like a normal person at school. The very first problem came when the teacher tried to force her to sit in a desk like everyone else.

Because she was not a person, Sandi was not allowed to sit at desks or tables. As they pushed her to sit at the table, she became increasingly agitated. When they finally tried to physically place her there, she erupted in screams. When released, once more told to sit at the desk, she picked it up as much as her slight weight and nonexistent strength would allow and heaved it bodily.

It was quite a feat that it managed an instant of being airborne before falling on its side and knocking another student out of his chair.

She ended up sitting in the back of the room. She was given something very special and unusual... crayons. They were colorful, bright, and cheerful. She scribbled until one of the other students taunted her about going outside the lines.

Coloring inside the lines was a fascinating idea. A strange and mystical concept she could only barely accept... the color was so exciting, but as she started to try to keep it inside the lines and could not do so, she became frustrated.

Agitated, she squatted over the coloring page, a basket of flowers which she was trying to make yellow, though she only knew what color it was because the teacher had told her, and pressed the crayon harder until it broke, sending her cowering into a corner in terror. Surely she would be terribly punished for breaking the pretty thing.

Time ticked on and no one seemed to care. No one beat her. No one kicked her. No one so much as spoke, they were all focused on the teacher, who seemed not to care at all. Creeping slowly, watching everyone around her, Sandi inched towards the calling crayons again, taking one crabbing step at a time.

She held onto one crayon desperately, trying to make her uncontrollable hand keep it inside the lines for yellow flowers. She lost all other thought, all other focus, her world narrowing to the crayon and her epic battle with the coloring page's lines.

When the teacher touched her gently on the shoulder to bring her to lunch, Sandi shrieked, her terror as much for her loss of awareness as the fear she had done something wrong. She sidled away, hiding under the desk that had been righted nearby, unoccupied.

She was given school lunch. They put it on the desk and told her that she could have it if she sat at the chair like a good girl.

She wasn't stupid. She knew all the tricks. She wasn't allowed human food and she wasn't allowed to sit at a table.

The crayon continued to confound her. The other student who was making fun of her came over and showed her how he held the crayons, telling her she was holding it wrong. She tried his way, but her fingers wouldn't work the way his did. It was awkward compared to holding it in her fist.

He colored, and his coloring stayed mostly in the area of the lines. She did note, however, that he also didn't get it right all the time. Some of his coloring was outside the lines. She decided not to tell him; she might get in trouble for backtalking a person. Especially a boy.

She fought again with the crayon and the lines. All around her on the walls of the school were pretty pictures. Bright, filled with color and magic, they obsessed her every time she went to a school.

As the day passed, the principle came for her. She followed him silently down the hallway, watching both directions for danger. They entered the school library, and he instructed her to wait there. She hid under a chair, watching and waiting, unaware of the change in routine—for she had no school routine to speak of.

The man came in then. He sat down at a table beside the one she squatted under. She soon heard the scritch-scritch of him drawing. Ever so slowly, carefully, she edged over to watch. She remembered the man very well, indeed.

"Donald!" She was delighted, and when he made the voice again, she laughed again, then silenced it, scared he would hit her.

He did not. "What would you like me to draw?"

"Armor-dirro."

He didn't understand. She knew he didn't understand. It frustrated her.

"Daddy hit one with the car," she tried to say, though it came out painfully garbled and strange. "It has armor on. If it gets scared, it curls up in a ball."

He did understand then. "An armadillo." He blinked at her. "You really want me to draw an armadillo?"

She nodded eagerly. It had been so cute, looked so sweet and small and funny. Before. Before Daddy, before the car... "Pweesh?"

He pulled a piece of paper over with a flourish and stretched his hands out as if he were about to do magic. "What the lady wants, the lady gets." He grinned at her, and she found her face trying to smile back and fought not to, looking away in case she met his eyes accidentally.

Pencil in hand, he began to make a circle. He talked about circles and squares, and how they could come together to create an armadillo. Circles were the base of many things, and she would have to learn to work with them if she wanted to make things like armadillos!

She crowded closer, watching these magical circle and square and rectangle things turn into something very like what she had seen. "His nose is too long," she corrected, and he seemed to understand.

"Oooh no," he said, heaving a heavy sigh. "I think I've made an anteater instead."

"And-deeder?" she tried to echo his word. "What's that?" She hated the way her mouth refused to make the right sounds.

"It's shaped like an armadillo, but it eats ants. Do you eat ants?"

She laughed. "Dno! Ub courd nod!" She was trying to say, 'No, of course not.' Her speech impediment made her sound like her mouth was full of food all the time, but she had no idea about such things, only that she didn't sound like everyone else.

He chuckled, "More for the anteater, I guess, right?"

She nodded vigorously. The anteater could have them all.

"I'll try again. Do you know where Mitch and Doris are right now?"

"Who?"

He seemed to think for a moment. "Your mom and dad. Do you know where they are right now?"

She shook her head, tugging on the paper. "Armor-dirro!"

He started drawing. "What about Marie? Do you know where she is?"

Sorrow welled up in her. "Dhe's gone'd."

"Gone where?"

She shrugged, eyes riveted to the paper. "Jus gone'd."

He asked her more questions, but she didn't want to get into trouble. She almost answered several times, because after all, she could trust the man, couldn't she? Yet she couldn't overcome it in herself and remained silent.

He drew the armadillo and she was sent back to class, where she remained for a time until general assembly was called. The kindergartners, which apparently meant her, were going to watch a movie. They were soon in the gymnasium, a massive space that made her both fascinated and terrified.

Soon, a projector was focused on the wall and a talking toothbrush appeared. He talked about things like enamel, and toothbrushing, and tartar and all sorts of peculiar things. Sandi didn't want to look away, but she had to keep track of the teacher who was moving around, talking to the other kids.

They were all sitting on the floor just like her.

She looked back up at the movie. She had never seen anything like it that she could remember except waking up once at a drive-in theatre with her mother and Jimmy. They had made her lay back down, so she hadn't been able to see anything more than two people running through the woods, taking their clothes off. They probably got bitten by ants...

The toothbrush and his friends, the tooth, the tube of toothpaste, and the dental tool ended the movie with a song and a dance. Then packets were handed out and they included small pink pills that the kids had to chew up.

They tasted terrible, but she got to see where she had missed while brushing her teeth, because the pink clung to the bad stuff. She had an awful lot of pink, and the teachers soon became annoyed with her driving need to get every tiny little bit of it with the toothbrush.

At 'home', the issue ended in a major struggle yet again. She was beaten and her toothbrush was taken.

Stupid animals didn't need toothbrushes, after all; only real people.

CHAPTER 27
NOBODY WANTS THEM, ANYWAY (DARREN)

DARREN HAD CAUGHT up with them. Each conversation with the kids had netted results, however slim, except Sandi's. He had struggled to understand her, which was enough on its own to render it barely productive, but she had also refused to answer anything that might have really helped him on his primary goal. She wouldn't speak about her mother aside from a word or two here and there.

She had admitted to frequent beatings, and had hinted at worse, but only in moments when her guard was down when distracted by him drawing. Her immense fascination with his drawings had made him stay longer with her than merited directly by his need for information.

"Did you hear?" he asked the social worker who sat beside him, prim and proper in her orange and tan pantsuit.

She pursed her lips. "Children often make things up, Mr. Burr. She clearly wanted to tell you what you wanted to hear."

He pinched the bridge of his nose. "She had no idea what I wanted to hear, and when did you get the idea that I wanted to hear that she was being beaten?"

She huffed slightly. "Children remember only the negative moments in things of this nature. You want her to believe she's being beaten and you want to believe it yourself. We have no idea where she got those bruises. If I told her she was being beaten, she'd remember being beaten even if she never had been. You really can't believe children. Intentionally or accidentally, they make things up."

His fist clenched harshly around the cane. He'd heard this sort of thing from endless people; you don't ask kids because kids always lie. When they don't lie or fabricate, they were probably coached. He hadn't had opportunity to coach any of these kids, the very idea was ludicrous.

"There's nothing we can do, Mr. Burr." Her voice was decisive, convinced, and gratingly nasal. "They don't appear to be in any danger, and we can't take them without probable cause." How could she think they were fine with Sandi was nothing but bones with a bit of skin on them?

Darren thanked her coldly for her time and left for the police station. Once there, he went inside to speak to the Lieutenant. He had an appointment.

Led inside the office, he sat down gratefully. The leg ached abominably at times, and this was one of them. It beat a steady warning that it was another town, another bust...

"I have a copy of the warrant for his arrest." Darren placed the warrant on the table. Mitch had raped one of his other foster daughters before fleeing. She had escaped and a warrant had been issued. It was on this warrant that Darren pinned his hopes of stopping Mitch.

The Lieutenant shook his head, not even glancing at it. "We don't have the manpower right now to serve someone else's warrant. Even if we did, we don't have an extradition agreement with Idaho."

"I have another warrant. This one is on the kids' behalf. It doesn't require extradition--"

He shook his head and stopped Darren again. "I'm very sorry, but we aren't the ones who would serve family court documents. That's the Sheriff's domain."

"They've already refused to serve it. Any officer of the law can--"

"Listen, Darren, I'm going to be straight with you. They live out there in the migrant area. Lot of migrants go through there. Mexicans and the like, you feel me?"

Darren scowled.

The other man sighed heavily. "It's dangerous. Those people, they police themselves. They are a law unto themselves. If we show up out there, it'll be a shootout to put the OK Corral to shame." He shook his head. "I just can't do it."

"Please." Darren wasn't above begging. He was desperate for help. "Look, everywhere they've gone, kids have gone missing. I talked to them today at the school and all of the kids said they're being beaten--"

"The social worker said--"

"She doesn't even believe kids know what's happening in their own lives, she doesn't know what she's doing--"

"She has worked with this department for years, Mr. Burr. She has a great track record and she really cares about kids. I think we're done here." He stood up and indicated the door with barest civility.

Darren gathered his warrants and hobbled from the room, his leg throbbing in a murderous beat. He stopped, almost begging again, but he'd learned it wouldn't do any good. Drooping with defeat, he turned to leave.

The kids were so close, and still a universe away. He had caught them, and it didn't mean a damned thing at all. Nobody wanted the headache. Mitch knew where to hide and how to avoid detection and police response. In Emmett, he had terrified the police and here, he simply lived in a place the police were terrified to go.

It was a nightmare and he was hopeless in the midst of it. He had played everything by the books, and still, day in and day out, he had to fight the very system that was supposed to help him and others. These kids needed him and they needed the systems that had been put in place to help them. They were left vulnerable and devastated because 'there's nothing you can do for those people'. He wanted to rant like a child in a grocery store isle who wanted a piece of candy and had just been told no.

He wanted to shout that it wasn't fair, but nobody would listen; nobody would care. "Life's not fair and there's nothing you can do to change that."

He returned to his hotel room and sat slumped in a chair, staring at the cane. It stared back, eyes hooded and accusing. He let his head fall onto the back of the chair. He wasn't big on kids, but he had made a commitment to their families, to them, and to himself. He wasn't going to give up.

Those poor kids. The little black girl's hair had started to come in since the incident weeks ago. She still looked forlorn and confused by the incident. The two boys had both been confrontational, the younger one even combative. They didn't like him, it was clear. They didn't trust him, either.

Kids that age, with that much rage and distrust... he shuddered to think of what the abuse they faced could do to them. The rage, he knew would get worse, and they would be destined for the streets. It was unthinkable and yet... it was inevitable unless they escaped.

He made it to the Mustang and returned again to the hotel, the world once more bleak and miserable.

It was no surprise when he woke the next day to find that they had gone again. They were always ahead of him; even when he had caught up to them.

CHAPTER 28
PUT THROUGH THE WRINGER – LITERALLY (SANDI)

SANDI WOKE UP from another dream where she was on the toilet. It was a common dream. Whenever she needed to potty at night, she would fall asleep and dream of being on the potty. Of course, as soon as she'd start to go, it would wake her up, wet and miserable.

She couldn't stop having the dream, and it got her beaten every time.

She silently gathered up her clothes and her sleeping rags. Gently, carefully, she crept along the hallway of their current place they shared with a bunch of other people. She got outside and put her clothes and sleeping rags in the bucket under the outdoor cistern pump.

It took everything she had to work the manual pump long enough for water to come out, then she fought it with all of her strength as it became even more difficult. Finally, she had enough water in the bucket to wash each item one by one.

The water was cold and the clothing was filthy from being unwashed for so long. It was hard work, but finally, she got it finished. The place they were staying had a clothes wringer. It was a new-fangled one with an electrical cord.

Sandi started trying to put her clothes through it, but she was terrified of the rolling wheels. Finally, in frustration, she left it running, tried to wring the clothes herself, and went back into the shelter. Dropping the wet rags on the floor, she put the still-dripping clothes back on.

When morning came, she was huddled on the wet rags on the floor. It took a good, long beating that time before she finally admitted all that had happened. She was dragged back through the shelter, everyone staring at her, with her wet rags clutched in her hand.

Outside, the machine still rattled and growled steadily. It had moved from its original position and now chugged away at the end of its electrical cord chain like a starved dog.

Doris dragged Sandi over to the machine, lifting her up to hold her between her own body and the machine. She handed her a rag and, holding her by the hair, forced her to start running the rags through the ringer.

The two rotating rollers had no way to feed or start the rags in between them, one simply had to be skilled at it. The greedy rollers would impartially grab anything that came close to them, smashing it forcefully together and 'wringing' or pressing the water out of it.

This mechanism worked fantastically for clothing; unfortunately, it was less helpful on arms. In a surely unpredictable stroke of either fate or carelessness, Sandi's finger was caught by the machine and pulled inwards.

Doris, being cleverer than the average bear, started pulling back the other direction whilst Sandi screamed bloody murder. The savage machine, indifferent to either, continued its inexorable marching roll, squeezing the two rubber-covered, hard rollers together against her arm.

Since it wasn't the first time Sandi had screamed that day, or that week, or that month, little notice was paid to the situation by others.

At this point, Doris decided that a more active role would be required, and went in search of help.

While the rollers continued to roll, and the machine continued to wobble, dangling Sandi before pulling her in far enough, her skin abraded from Doris's pulling, that she was now draped across the water basin and now was up to her shoulder in the rollers.

Rollers rolled. Rubber chafed. Skin burned. Sandi screamed. The rollers got closer and closer to her face before a passing worker saw and yanked the cord out of the wall.

It was eternity before they finally figured out how to remove the housing and disconnect the top roller enough to free Sandi's arm.

The beating for humiliating Doris was quite severe. Doris received much comforting for having to put up with 'the retard' who had stuffed her arm into a wringing machine. Life, of course, was a great trial for poor Doris. Her plight so horrible, her suffering so tremendous, that she feared she might have a breakdown.

Sandi hid in terror, her arm burning with a raging fire, her skin agonized, while the women in the shelter comforted Doris with great compassion.

"It must have been so frightening for you to see your poor little girl trapped like that."

"You're a wonderful mother, so patient and understanding."

"It must be so hard. I don't think I could do it."

And so the comments went until the conversation moved on to Doris's recent tragic miscarriage. The other women in the group gave her small comfort items, shampoo, hair dye, chocolates, candies, and various other items to help her relax through her terrible grief and suffering.

Sandi did not eat that night in punishment for her stupidity. The next morning, they took off again, always on the run. They were making for the East Coast, where Mitch was going to show his beautiful wife the eastern ocean. She wanted it and so she would have it, for she deserved to have whatever she wanted.

CHAPTER 29
ALWAYS A LOCAL MATTER (DARREN)

"JUST HEAR ME out, please. I need help. I've been tracking these people for months. I've got proof that everywhere they go, kids disappear--"

"But you have no proof that they were the ones who made the kids disappear, by your own admission."

Darren wanted to scream. He wanted to throw the phone. He wanted to throttle the man on the other end. "I have a warrant from Idaho and a writ of Habeus Corpus--"

"That's not a matter for the FBI, man. We have important cases to look into. Real criminals that we know are hurting people. I can dig that this is a real big thing for you--"

"I met with the kids at the last town. They are being badly abused--" Frustration built as the was cut off mid-sentence yet again by the jackass on the other end.

"Which you said the social worker didn't agree was the case."

"Alright," Darren conceded. "What do you need from me to get you to help me with this case?"

"Get me proof that they are disappearing kids, man, and I'll get all over it. Until then, we got nothin'." The phone's click and following dial tone spoke volumes more than the agent himself had. 'Screw you.'

The next call went almost as poorly. Another police department, another sheriff's office... another no, another 'not our business' another 'understaffed' or another 'sorry, too dangerous'.

Now, in that state of discouragement, he had to call his dad. Great, just great.

"Yeah?" the voice on the other end of the line was familiar, brusque, and deepened by years of smoking. He had quit now, but his dad had smoked for years.

"Dad, it's Darren."

"Heey son," he drawled the first word. "I have a feelin' you aren't on your way home right now."

"Dad, I caught up with them. I found them and I caught up with them."

"So why aren't you on your way home, then?" Leave it to Dad to be reasonable and level-headed.

"I still can't get anyone to help me, and if I just take them, I'll be the one to land in jail."

"Well, that's quite a pickle, son. What're you going to do?" His voice somehow managed to convey, 'since it's clear you're not going to pack up and come home like I told you to'.

He groaned and dropped his head into his other hand, running it through his hair. "I dunno. I need help, Dad. I can't just keep hoping I'll find someone who'll understand and help me. It hasn't worked so far, and I really doubt it's going to change anytime soon."

"You're right, kid, it isn't." He took a deep breath and blew it out.

"Are you smoking again, Dad?" Darren was distracted for a moment.

"Nope, but if you keep this shit up, I'm going to end up smoking like a chimney. You're driving yourself to ruin on this wild goose chase." He paused again to reflect. "Here's what you gotta do, Darren. Catch them at something the local authorities do care about and something you can prove. It won't be the win you're looking for.

You can't prove the murders, and you can't prove the kidnapping so long as no one's willing to listen and help. So find something on them that matters locally."

"How the hell am I supposed to do that?"

"You'll figure it out, son. You're sure as hell motivated enough." Another pause. "How much do you need this time?"

Darren told him, naming a figure under what he really thought he needed. His father swore vociferously on the other end, but the money was at a neighboring town that had a wire transfer station by noon the next day.

CHAPTER 30
MOVIE MAGIC (SANDI)

DIFFERENT SCHOOL, same scene; Sandi refused to sit at a table or eat human food. No amount of enticement would work, yet again. She knew what would happen if she sat at that table, and she wasn't about to volunteer for it.

It was the same each time. Every school tried to break her of the habit; when she did get to go to school at all, that was. Mitch and Doris often argued that she shouldn't go to school, but in some areas, it was mandatory, in spite of Sandi's status as 'a retard'.

This particular place required it and she was back at school, squatting in the back of class and trying to color. This time, another boy had joined her, and they were able to understand each other somewhat, talking in quiet whispers or simply handing each other things they wanted without even having to think about it.

She was contentedly drawing armadillos and yellow flowers all over every paper when the general assembly bell rang and everyone, including she, were herded into a large room with stadium seating. She squatted in the back of the room while her new friend went and sat down, waving good-bye with sad eyes.

She wanted to sit next to him so badly that tears ran down her face, but she did and said nothing. She would be punished, and so would he. No, she would sit here, alone, as always.

As she waited, the room grew quiet and dark, and a movie began. She was astonished. It was beautiful. Photo-perfect pictures this time, no dancing toothbrushes or animated teeth... real pictures of real people moving around. It was fascinating and she soon moved up to sit on the cold concrete step instead of squatting at the back of the room.

The movie was called Gus, and it seemed like magic to her. The mule was the man's friend. He was on the man's side and helped him. The people's clothes were incredibly fancy, and they all lived in mansions.

She had seen TV on the tiny little black-and-white TV, in the rare times she was even allowed to see it while it was on. This gigantic image, however, captivated her. The beauty of the homes, the perfect hair on the women, and men wearing suits (not that she knew what suits were, only that they were oh-so-fancy).

For just a moment, she dared to dream of being in nice clothes and being around people in nice clothes, and having a life like that. The momentary surge of desire was immediately squashed. Such things were not now, and never would be for someone like her.

On the other hand, there was Gus. The mule was a loyal friend, a staunch supporter. Merely an animal, he was smart and clever and unfailing in his loyalty. She wanted that. She laughed at the same times others did, even though she almost never understood what was funny or why.

But behind it all was the desire for a loyal friend. As she left the room, she kept looking back, hoping that Gus would be there on the screen. Of course, he wasn't. He wasn't even real. None of it was real.

She had no interest in food that night and bore the beating for being wasteful in stony silence. She did her chores without interest and with no care of whether she did it right or not. It didn't matter to her when she was beaten again for disobedience when she didn't move quickly enough.

None of it really mattered. Every friend she ever had died or went away. There was no Gus... there was no puppy... there was no one at all. Just this life, forever. No one even cared what happened to her. She wasn't even allowed to die.

She huddled in on herself and stared at the papers on the floor, crayons scattered over them. Not even this mattered.

That night and for many after, she lay and imagined she had a friend. When the daydreams ended and her life returned, it was harder than before. She cared less and tried less, taking the beatings with a resignation that she had never experienced before.

CHAPTER 31
DARREN TAKES SCORE (DARREN)

DARREN HAD CAUGHT up to them again. It really meant little, because he hit the same walls he had always hit. Little Rock, Arkansas was the same. The local Sheriff was sympathetic, which was a step up, but admitted that he wouldn't be allowed to act without the permission of the Prosecuting Attorney; it was he who would be required to act upon the extradition request.

The PA had been, at best, disinterested.

Darren went back to the Sheriff. Leaning back in his chair, the man had considered for a time. "Well, if the PA's office isn't going to help you, maybe we can find something on them. If they're as bad as you say, I suspect that if we keep an eye on them, we can catch them at something.

"I'll tell you what. I'll have a couple of my boys help keep an eye on them. They'll be discreet. It does no good for them to see cops and take off. Street clothes, and their own cars, I think. I want to help. I can't stand to see kids going through this kind of thing. If he really raped that girl, he needs to be put away for a very long time. I know my boys will feel the same way."

Darren stood now on the street outside the grocery store, his heart leaden and his hope and money both fading fast. He had some hope, at least, but the Sheriff had made it clear that they couldn't act on what Darren had alone. He was out of money and out of options and when he finally found someone willing to help, it was too little, too late.

It was by merest chance that he looked up at the gas station across the way from him. He noticed the white truck sitting there; new, with an ancient and unkept camper on it. As his gaze slid past, it snapped back, a frisson of excitement running up his spine.

Was that Mitch Jones getting out of that truck? There was no way it could be. It was too much to hope for. It was nigh on impossible.

Sure enough, Mitch had gotten out of the truck and was starting to pull the nozzle from the gas pump.

His father's words whispered through his mind, and Darren knew that, if he played his cards right, he would have Mitch now. "Get them for something else."

No way in hell Mitch could afford that truck unless it was stolen. He was completely certain that he had him now. He had him and he wouldn't let him go even one town further. It wasn't the win he wanted, no. Mitch wouldn't pay for what he had done, no. Yet the most important thing would be accomplished; he would get those kids away from him.

Darren lifted the camera he kept around his neck as Mitch took off, not paying for the gas. The station attendant ran out, enraged and shouting.

The camera hadn't caught the license plate, but thanks to the zoom on it, Darren had. The photo wouldn't be readable because the vehicle was moving when he took the photo, but Darren had captured it mentally.

He wrote it down and rushed to the Sheriff's office, his hands trembling. Come to find out, as he had suspected, the truck was stolen.

The Sheriff smiled. It wasn't a pretty smile. It was a smile two predators shared as they closed in on their prey. Darren smiled back.

It was time. All he had to do was find out where they were living. It turned out that it wasn't as easy as it seemed at first.

"We'll go get them for you, my man," the Sheriff told him once they had figured out where the family was staying.

"Thank you." As the other man moved to assemble his team, Darren stopped him, "Tell your guys to let the little girl come to them, and that she only eats food off of the floor. I know it's bizarre, but they've been badly abused. Just... let her come to you."

The Sheriff nodded. "We'll do that, son." He squeezed Darren's shoulder before heading out.

Darren walked to the courthouse to wait. The cold marble floor made his hip ache as he paced back and forth, back and forth. At last, he had to sit down on a cold, hard bench for the interminable wait. He looked through the toys and things he had brought. He hoped the kids would like them. He didn't know much about kids, they weren't exactly his most comfortable demographic.

CHAPTER 32
REST AND REUNION
(DARREN & SANDI)

THE PIGS WERE there. The Fuzz. Coppers. Sandi hid in terror. Pigs meant danger. They would take her away from Mommy and Dad, and then they'd torture her, and nobody could protect her from them except Mommy and Dad. And Mommy and Dad had promised to kill anyone who took Sandi away from them. No one was safe. They had told her so. Even if the pigs wanted to help her, they couldn't. They were the evil oppressors. The Man. The Man wanted to control everyone and take away freedom.

She cowered under the table. They had tried once to get her to come out, but she was no fool. She knew far better than to do that. They'd hurt her. They'd steal her.

Silence fell for a long time, and she finally looked out. The pig sat on the floor, eating something. He looked up as she peeked out, and he pushed something on the ground towards her. "This is yours." He went back to eating, saying nothing more.

She crept out a single crab-stepping shuffle. He didn't move. Adults were fast, though, so you had to be careful. A few more steps brought her closer to the food. It smelled really nice, and her stomach was pinched with the fire of hunger.

She got close and grabbed the food, scrambling away in case it was a trap.

Unfazed, the pig sat eating his own food. When he was done, he took out a book and started reading. Out loud. She listened, not moving from her hiding spot for what felt like forever.

He put another piece of whatever the food was on a plate and scooted it towards her silently. She'd never had pizza, so couldn't identify it.

His voice grew softer, and she crept slowly forward, straining to listen. She sat next to him after a while and ate, still wary, still jumping several feet away every time he moved. She finished every bite of the food, and her stomach protested. She vomited, embarrassed.

It didn't seem to matter to the pig at all. He just went back to reading. She inched forward after trying to clean up her mess with a towel. His voice got quieter and she got closer.

He stopped reading and looked at her. His face was kind, not mean. It was confusing.

"There's a friend who would like to see you. He drew these for you, so you would remember him." He showed her a piece of paper with Mickey and Donald on it. "Would you like to go see him?"

She nodded. He stood up slowly and held his hand out. She took it after a long contemplation. He waited patiently.

She sat beside him in the police cruiser. He turned the lights on for her, and she laughed with delight. She clapped her hands over her ears when he turned on the siren, her eyes huge and shocked... "Again!" She laughed. It was a wonderful feeling.

Then they were there. They walked up the stairs to a giant building that looked like a school. "Amb I unger arreft?" she asked. She must be under arrest, because it wasn't quite like a school, and he was a pig who stole children. She didn't really care anymore, though. She liked 'pizza' and maybe he would beat her less than Doris and Mitch.

"No," he replied. "You didn't do anything wrong, sugar. I only arrest people who do bad things, and you seem pretty nice to me."

"I dun tink uurr... yer... ur a pig ad all." She still couldn't make her words form right.

He seemed to understand, though. "The only people who think I'm a pig is my wife because I don't pick up my dirty socks, and bad people who I have to arrest. So I agree with you, I don't think I'm a pig, either." He held the door open and winked at her, "Because I pick up some of my socks."

She followed him with a slight smile. Her foster sister Maureen, her foster brother Ronnie, and her half-brother James were there. The policeman opened a door and shooed them into the next room.

The man was there. The man who had visited her twice and who drew pictures for her. He really was there. He had come to see her again.

The four of them crowded him, hugging him and laughing.

The others started looking through the toys, and Sandi knew she wouldn't get to until later. She would be last, she was always last. She watched the man draw pictures. He let her sit on his lap, and she fell asleep, trusting for the first time in years that she was safe.

CHAPTER 33
THE CALLING (DARREN & SANDI)

THE KIDS WERE to be taken into protective custody. They would not be going back to the Joneses. They were free now. Mitch had been arrested at his workplace for receiving stolen property. Doris had been arrested at the 'family home', which was little more than a shack made of plywood and roofing tar.

Whatever they had seen there, the deputies were reluctant to speak on it. They all made it plain, however, that there was no way in hell those kids were going back. Photographs had to be made of the kids, their bodies covered in welts and scars and bruises.

The worst of all was Sandi. Her ribs protruded, even her pelvis protruded so much that he could have fit a thumb between it and her belly. Her eyes were sunken and she looked exhausted.

All of them ran into his arms, hugging him, laughing and holding on. Four months of pure hell had culminated in that moment. Four starving, weary kids running into his arms. He looked into their happy faces and he had to turn away as tears sprang to his eyes and overflowed. He'd been taught not to cry, that it was weakness, but it felt like joy to him. It felt like winning.

He held Sandi as she slept against him, guessing it was a rare and special moment in her life; knowing it was a rare and special one in his own. Her tiny, frail, starved body felt as light as a feather and he wanted to hug her close, but she felt fragile, as if she might break if he even breathed.

As the social workers gathered the children up to go to their temporary homes, he felt a surprising sorrow that he had to watch them go. They were hustled away, their new toys going with them. He gathered himself up to follow in their wake.

There were things to do, like explain to his dad that he still wasn't on his way home yet, and he needed more money to get there.

He looked down at the cane, his great nemesis—his new best friend.

"Okay, you were right. I don't really hate kids. I might even think the little buggers are alright." As he, and his cane, emerged into the sunlight, he knew that this had been a defining journey in his life. He was forever altered. He could only hope that the lives of those children were, as well.

When he got home several days later, and had slept the long drive off, he went for a walk. He wandered aimlessly, contemplating his life and what his next steps should be in his newly realized passion to save children, when he found himself outside his favorite tat shop.

He laughed and looked down at the cane. "Was this your idea?" It was, of course, silent. Chuckling at his own whimsy, he said, "Well, let's go, then."

All of his tats had meaning and purpose behind them. These four... well, these four would be no different. He would always remember, and if he ever, for a moment, considered forgetting, these tats would remind him.

He pushed open the door and walked in. Settling in the chair after making his choices, his tat-master asked, "So what is it this time?"

Sighing, he leaned back and began to tell the story of the

predator he had hunted for four grueling months. When he told about the kids running into the room, he realized that everyone in the shop had come over to listen and there wasn't a dry eye in the house.

The time came that he had to go see his dad and give his accounting. He went, repayment check in hand, cringing at the amount.

"Hey, Dad," he said into the office.

His dad looked up, and Darren thought he looked tired and a little defeated. "Come on in, son."

Darren told the story. Then he showed his dad the photos of the abuse the kids had experienced and their sorry state upon being rescued.

His dad got up and came around the desk, giving him a rare, swift, hard embrace; the hug of an old-school father for his son. "I'm proud of you, Darren."

Darren saw tears starting in his father's eyes, and he was moved to near tears, himself. It was a moment of vulnerability, and he understood it all too well.

"Now get out of here and get back to work, you lazy cuss." As his dad settled down into his chair, he added, "And leave that check."

Darren chuckled. "It's right there, Dad."

With that, Darren went back to work for his Dad, with a new determination that he would find a way to help kids. Many ways, if he could. In the meantime; he had to eat and his father needed the help.

The pain of the fresh tattoos made him smile. They would always be there to remind him.

_____ # THE END #_____

Q&A
COMMON QUESTIONS ABOUT THE STORY

Q. Why did you write the book in third person when it's your own story?

A. Because I needed the effort of translating it from first to third person. That helped give me a focus beyond the agony and the horrible memories. I write far better in third person, and I like third person a lot more than first person. Let's be honest, that could be fixed with an edit, though. It was very, very much because I needed the 'distraction' of switching points of view. Writing this book took me to an extremely dark place and without that necessary 'step back', I don't think I would have survived the writing. That, by the way, is also why it's not edited. I tried and tried to edit it. I finally got a wonderful editor, but I realized that I just couldn't edit it. I couldn't do my part on the edit. I hope that people will find it in themselves to forgive me for that.

Q. Where did you (Sandi) end up?

A. I went to live with my Maternal grandparents in Kansas a year after being rescued in November of 1978 in Little Rock, Arkansas.

. . .

Q. Was it better than the Joneses?

A. Yes, of course it was better; it wouldn't take much of anything to be better than there. It was dysfunctional by almost any standard (except perhaps the Joneses and any like them), but it was truly a gigantic leap up. I will never be anything but tremendously grateful to have escaped from the Jones' home.

Q. How did Mitch and Doris get custody of you?

A. This is really uncertain. The only part I've been told clearly is that my mother went to jail for prostitution and possession. At that time, Mitch and Doris came forward to my mother as wonderful, loving foster parents; we were given to them either by my mother or the court. The truth is likely to remain unknown forever. I was 3 at the time they got hold of us.

Q. How did your mother know Mitch and Doris?

A. They are supposedly related. I say supposedly because no one is able to answer my questions on the subject without debate and speculation. According to the sources I most trust (least reason to bother lying), my mother is Doris's half-sister. The story goes that my grandmother gave birth to Doris first, but left her behind to be raised as if she were my mother's aunt/ my grandmother's youngest sister. The stigma against unwed pregnancy would have ruined my grandmother's social climb (through marriage), so had to be covered up.

Q. Did you really see your mother being sawed up and fed to pigs?

A. I remember it very clearly, indeed. There has been enough supporting evidence since to convince me that I really did see it. Not enough (as of the writing of this book) to convict in court, sadly.

. . .

Q. WHAT HAPPENED to the other known foster kids in the home?

A. At the time that we were on the run, there was me, James, Ronnie, and Maureen. James is fine, living his life and prefers his privacy. I beg all to leave him be, he has suffered enough and wishes to be left alone. Ronnie passed away while playing chicken with a train while he was drinking. Maureen still lives with Doris and prefers her privacy as well, as far as I know.

Q. What about any other foster kids who weren't on the run?

A. I know about Kevin, who was removed from the home and sent to a boy's home before we went on the run; about Roy, who is a serial killer on death row; and about Katrin, who was the girl Mitch raped and who passed away from cancer some years ago. Katrin had escaped from them and Mitch was charged with 'incest' for his brutal rape of her. He did serve time for it; not much. He got 5 years and served 3. Out on 'good behavior'.

Q. WHAT TIME did Mitch and Doris serve for what they did to you?

A. None. Mitch did a very small bit of time for 'incest' for raping Katrin. Nothing of any kind has been done about anything else.

Q. WHERE ARE they (Mitch and Doris) now?

A. They are long since divorced and live separate lives. Both live pretty nearby Emmett. As of the completion of this book, I have been told both have died, but interestingly enough there are rumors that Mitch is not dead. It was a police officer who told me he was, so I suppose I shall assume he's dead; yet the police in that area are not entirely trustworthy in my personal opinion.

· · ·

Q. How do you know what Darren went through to be able to write it into your story?

A. I don't. I chose to turn Darren's character into a fictionalized account because I really needed the viewer to see all the struggles he faced, without writing in 4-6 months' worth of frustration, desperation, and encounters. Perhaps someone else will do a better job of that. I certainly hope so, as it's a fascinating case from any angle. He is also a conglomerate character where I placed some knowledge which wasn't gathered by him, but by other reputable investigative individuals (police and prosecutors, detectives, etc.).

Q. Was your part of the story fictionalized, too?

A. It is pretty much as accurate as I could make it, with the caveat that a lot of incidents were ongoing, repetitious, and quite difficult to relate over and over again with their minor differing details. For example, the beatings, the strangling, the curling irons, the sexual violence... all frequent and common. The scene where she tried to make me break the ice and take a bath in the frozen pond was an event that wasn't repeated. So while my parts were at times a combination of similar events, they were kept as honest and true as I could manage.

Q. Where is your dad through all of this?

A. It's hard to say for absolute certain. The man who was married to my mother at birth was definitely not my father. He repudiated me repeatedly until I was an adult. I don't precisely care to know. There is some speculation that my mother's father (my grandfather) may be my father.

Q. What? How do you feel about that?

A. I don't really care. I understand that some will look down on me for it, but at the end of the day, my personal view is that there's nothing I can do about it. I wasn't there, I didn't get to choose. I'm not like those people; I chose who I would be, instead. After all I've been through, this just seems like no big deal to me. Perhaps it's time we destigmatize things that are out of the person's control, anyway.

Q. How long were you with them (the Joneses)?

A. Four years or so. I'm uncertain on the exact months, but I came to them at age 3, my mother disappeared right after my 6th birthday, and I was rescued right after my 7th birthday. I was in foster care for a year before going to my grandparents' home.

Q. So you don't seem to be 'retarded'...

A. It's not really that simple. I do have a speech impediment, which I have overcome to a degree that no one guesses it ever existed. This fueled the belief that I was 'retarded'. However; I was diagnosed low functioning autistic when I was 9. I also have, I believe, overcome this at least on a social level. I still have numerous symptoms that I must deal with for myself every day. I just hide them as well as I can. I was told by a therapist that it may well be that my 'symptoms' are simply a result of the abuse I suffered, and likely caused by some of the damage done to me during those years.

Q. How is it that you're not royally screwed up beyond words?

A. Because someone once told me the most important thing I've ever heard; "You get to choose what kind of person you'll be. If you want to be a good person, be a good person."

Q. So your life is great now, right?

A. People really want me to tell them the fairy tale. The fact is that I'm pretty normal by most people's standards. This would seem to most to be a bad or sad thing, but keep in mind how far behind I came from. Reaching 'normal' with 'normal problems' was a massive slog for me. I choose to be proud of myself for even making it this far. No, I'm not a war hero. Life hasn't "compensated me" for the evil things that were done to me. This is not a just world. There's no pie-in-the-sky magic ending for me yet.

Q. WHAT EFFECT has all this had on you in the long term?

A. It's impossible for me to know, of course, as I have no basis of comparison. I'm certain I have PTSD (at minimum), cPTSD, and I've struggled with anxiety disorders, extreme insomnia, depression, suicidal feelings and the like all my life. I've had a hard time forming relationships (could be my autism, too, though). I've struggled to hold down a job, also. I've chosen not to get involved with drugs or alcohol, but I might enjoy online gaming more than might be *altogether* healthy.

Q. HAVE YOU GOTTEN COUNSELING?

A. Yes, at times I have. Unfortunately, it always felt like the counselors were titillated (sexually stimulated) by my recounting of events, and morbidly fascinated. This made me uneasy and felt like it was making things worse. When I started writing this, I was seeing a therapist, but he put me into group therapy, and to be blunt, those people can't help me. Therapy has not helped me. I have become jaded to where I think there may just be no help for me. Which is fine, I'm getting by. Really. I do fine for a normal person, which means I do exceptional in the lens of my experiences.

Q. With your family history do you think that it was nature or nurture that can create serial killers like your foster brother?

A. It's important that I note, this question is because Roy is on death row, a convicted serial killer who murdered three people. You can look up Ramon Jones murderpedia if you're curious.

I would say that it can be either one; or a combination of both. The other boys there, that we know of, did not become serial killers. I know one of them was far more brutally abused than the one on death row. Why did one become one, and the rest did not? Granted, the other boy got away sooner, so it's not definitive.

The 'fosters' absolutely groomed all the boys to be killers. They were forced to kill animals, and often to torture them. Whether it was the sadistic pleasure of watching sensitive boys do things that hurt their own hearts, or whether it was truly (as claimed) intended to 'toughen them up', I cannot really know. I do know that it was common for them to be encouraged to have pets--then be forced to slaughter them as food or to simply kill them if they were dogs or cats, etc.. I think that would beak many a person's psyche.

Q. Do you still have any ties to that side of the family?
A. I do not have ties to any of my family at all. I was removed from my grandparents' home at 15, and I never looked back except *very* briefly around age 23. I was suicidal within days and realized I had no choice but to flee.

Q. How was life when you finally got away from all that?
Life was still very hard when I got away from them, but it's sort of the difference between a snowstorm versus a full-on whiteout blizzard. Either way, you know the s-word is coming down... but there was a lot less of it after that. If that PI hadn't saved me, I am completely certain I would be dead--murdered by those people. I remember them murdering multiple children.

I was in foster care for a year while court stuff happened. I was badly abused in almost all of them. When I finally got to my grandparents (mothers' parents), I was horribly traumatized. Or, in their words, "a difficult child". My grandparents and the other kids in the home hated and blamed me. It's hard to like, much less love, an extremely terrified and reactive child. It's easy to assume it can be done, but as I've grown older I've begun to realize that they also got the raw end of a very raw deal.

I was thought mentally challenged (a retard, in the vernacular of the time). As an autistic person, I was badly abused by the school for the few years I was in 'special education', and I experienced significant difficulties overcoming a speech impediment by myself without any help or guidance of any kind. I also have dyslexia and scoliosis, mostly stemming from birth defects due to my mother drinking and doing drugs heavily while pregnant. She also tried to use various herbs and potions to abort me, as it wasn't legal at the time.

Ironically, I look normal if you don't know these things, so it was hard for people to understand how it was that I couldn't "act right".

I do believe that, at least in our current and that time frame's paradigm, I probably got the best that could be hoped for... which is a very sorry fact, indeed. We as a society need to do much, much better.

Q. And are there any articles I can read about this?

A. As of this writing, there are only the Thin Air Podcast episodes about her. Thinairpodcast.com and Marie Ann Watson (Season One). There are three. I have also created a subreddit where I have housed as much information as I could. There are newspaper clippings and what paltry evidences I could gather up there. www.reddit.com/r/MarieAnnWatson is the address.

Q. Did they look into what happened to your mother?

A. At the time, they did not. In fact, it was quite casually blown off. "You know how *those people* are" was the attitude. You know, whores and druggies, who cares?

In 1994, however, when Ramon (Roy) was arrested with 2 dismembered bodies in his storage area, the police came to visit me. There was some fear I might be one of the bodies. At that time, I basically said, "Let me tell you where he learned [about dismembering people]..."

In 1996, after that case completed, the first real investigation by authorities was launched into my mother's disappearance. Unfortunately, the bones they found at the time came back "inconclusive" (human or animal?), and so the investigation lost steam and petered out.

Q. WHAT IS your happiest memory from your childhood?

A. From that time? It would have to be when Katrin left. She is the one who was raped, by the way. All of the kids got silver dollars from the bus driver, except me. I wasn't in school yet.

When she left, she gave me that silver dollar to bribe me to stay in bed while she ran away. It was the only present I ever got during that time, and it was extra precious because I had wanted it so very, very badly. It's important to understand that I was not considered a person by those people. I ate dog food on the floor with 'the other stupid animals' because they thought I was retarded (and they loathed me; apparently they hated me because of hate for my mother transferred onto me).

Not from that time? Well... more complex an answer. Any time I got to spend with "my" horse on the farm I lived on with my grandparents. She was a beautiful appaloosa and I really thought she was mine until they sold her. Also, the time I spent with the family dog, a beautiful black labrador.

. . .

Q. At such a young age, how did you react to everything? Could you really comprehend it all?

A. I comprehended more than people give kids credit for... yet there were other things that I simply couldn't understand. This is a tough question to answer, because it's sort of broad. If you don't mind, I'll speak to a couple of things, and hope they answer your question adequately.

For example, I did know my mother was dead. When I saw her in his arms, with her head at a strange angle, I knew she was dead. I was beyond devastated. I absolutely and completely knew she was dead, and admittedly, my predominant thoughts were a bit selfish; I would never be rescued, I would never be hugged again... Yet at the same time, I had tried to 'save' her a few days earlier (as I recall, could have been more than a few days, hard to say with childhood memories).

The foster 'mother' had told me that if anyone tried to take me away, they'd kill her. I tried to convince my mother to take me and just run away where they couldn't find us, to save herself from them. She, of course, couldn't by court order.

However; the problem I had understanding it all was that, once my mother died, I genuinely had no concept that anything or anyone else could rescue us. Once she was gone, I truly believed that was forever... I'd *never* be free.

It was 4 years of hell. I did understand permanence, but I did NOT understand impermanence. Once I believed myself trapped, I believed myself trapped forever. I had no concept that I'd grow up, that was in some dim, will-never-get-here future.

With regards to the abuse, I didn't really question things. I had no basis of comparison, and they told me I was a stupid animal. I couldn't grasp any of that, quite frankly. I knew I wasn't... but yet I didn't. It was a very strange dichotomy that I still sometimes experience. I'm intelligent... no I'm not or it wouldn't have been so much work to seem intelligent... back and forth. Apparently, there are some things I still don't 'get'!

. . .

Q. How did your mind cope with it?

A. I compartmentalized. Also, I frequently personalized inanimate objects.

Q. Did you normalize it? Children often do, to the point that they might play "pretend" with themes of what is going on in their lives. It often disturbs adults.

A. I would not say I did this. As an autistic person, I'm very literal. Far less so now than I was as a child. I did, however, have an active imagination, it simply had nothing to do with what was happening to me. I could not mingle fantasy and reality (still can't very well, takes a ton of effort--I am not the best to play pretend with my child when they were little, but I do try!).

I did like to tell stories during my years with my grandparents. However, they were outrageous and based on stories that others read to me. I just assumed they would understand I was repeating the same stories. I thought them saying it wasn't true was a game. I mean... they had read me the story! How could they think I was serious? I didn't understand until years and years later that not everyone's memory is as good as mine. They actually didn't remember reading me those stories. It was very strange to me.

Q. Did anyone at school ever notice anything different about you or any of the other kids you lived with?

A. People noticed. I was thought to be 'a retard' and so all my, er, eccentricities... were attributed to that. Otherwise, it was a different time. If people beat their kids, it was considered normal and it was a very "mind your own business, ALWAYS, in ALL things" time. The few who did report it were completely ignored, often even told off.

"Social services are overburdened. Stop wasting our time. If it's not severe, they'll survive." Oh, the irony.

Q. How does your mind cope with everything now?

A. I find that I still compartmentalize. As an autistic person, I am not able to disassociate, but I am able to simply set things aside and to split them into their own categories. Not everything, mind you, but most things.

As I wrote the book, I found myself becoming increasingly horrified as I realized, for the first time, the true starkness and horror of that entire time period. 4 years of being brutally tortured, of eating dog food, of being thought not a person (brain capacity of a dead turtle, according to them).

I only began to realize how relentless it really was. I realized I spent 4 years of my childhood without a single present, birthday cake, hug (except a few from my mother on visitations), etc. Being beaten for anything and everything... it was really, really hard.

Intellectually, I knew it was genuinely horrible, but I hadn't really looked at it as a cohesive whole before. Terribly, unspeakably stark.

Q. Are you ever afraid that you might have picked something up from that experience which makes you similar to the people you lived with?

A. Less now than when I was young, and than when I first had my child. Most of my life, though, I heard how I *HAD TO* become like them, because *EVERYONE* who has gone through that, does... It's hard to stand in the face of that coming at you from every direction. Experts were quick to tell me that I HAD to be an addict, alcoholic, *something*.

A teacher once told me, "You get to decide what kind of person you're going to be. Nobody else." BEST. WORDS. EVER. Saved my life.

• • •

Q. How did you end up where you are today?

A. I just survived mostly. I decided when I was 8 years old that I was going to become "so normal" that no one would know how many medical issues, mental issues, negative life experiences, etc. I had. Now I joke that I clearly set my sights way too low.

Q. Have you come to terms with all these incidents?

A. Most of the time. I chose to embark on a path of radical self-forgiveness a few years ago. I have made exponential progress since then. I found I held a lot of guilt about things that were completely not my fault. As I dealt with that, it gave me tremendous peace.

To David, and Carol and Dave, to Jane, to Nancy; the closest thing I have to family right now.

To Matt and Colleen Viter and their girls, who gave me a home and love and kindness and dignity in a time when I felt I didn't have any of that.

To my friend Josh, who has been here through the ordeal of writing this book. Thank you for your kindness, your love, your understanding. Thank you for not freaking out. Thanks for believing me even after you were told to "take [my] little stories about [my] mother with a bucket of salt".

Definitely for my child, who is my reason to live. For my new child who I've brought into my life by design instead of birth.

And, of course, to all (such as the man who fed me all those years ago) who have taken time out of their busy lives for kindness to me; for those who take that time for anyone in the world. To all the kind people who don't let others dissuade them. All who are sneered at for compassion, caring, and protectiveness but who persevere with it anyway.

Clearly, it goes without saying, but of course to my own personal Hero, Darren Burr, who did not let anything stop him and who is the reason I'm still alive, 40 years later, to even write this book. The Detective in the story is predominantly based on him.

My sincerest thanks to vcdone for the cover, and to all who offered to edit and/or proofread for me.

Made in United States
Troutdale, OR
03/22/2025